Life in the workhouse: the story of Milton Union, Kent

Helen Allinson

SYNJON BOOKS

ISBN 0 904 373 09 6

Published by Synjon Books 2005

Copyright© Helen Allinson 2005

Helen Allinson has asserted her rights under the Copyright Designs and Patents Act, 1988 to be identified as the author of this work.

All Rights Reserved

This book is sold subject to the condition that no part of it may be reproduced, stored in a retrieval system, or transmitted, in any form or by any means, without the prior permission in writing of the publisher, nor be circulated in any form of binding or cover other than that in which it is published and without a similar condition including this condition being imposed on the subsequent purchaser.

Synjon Books
5, Homestead View,
The Street, BORDEN,
Sittingbourne, Kent,
ME9 8JQ

For details of other publications see our website:
http://www.synjonbooks.co.uk

For Barry

Acknowledgements

Thanks are due to the staff at Sittingbourne Local Studies Library for the cheerful and friendly way in which they always helped with my enquiries. Thanks too to the staff at the Centre for Kentish Studies for their courteous efficiency.

Many people in Milton and Sittingbourne have been kind enough to share their memories of the workhouse and hospital with me and given me invaluable first hand information about the institution in its later years.

My husband Barry has been a critical but encouraging reader as have my parents, John and Dorothea Teague and without the computer skills of my brother Tony Teague, I would still be struggling to format the book for printing.

CONTENTS

Acknowledgements	4
Introduction	7
PART ONE	9
The setting up the Union Workhouse 1834-1835	9
The Riots	13
The Workhouse Building	18
PART TWO - 1835-1900	26
Admission and Discharge	27
Work Inside the Workhouse	31
Discipline in the Early Years	36
The School in the Workhouse	40
Bread and Cheese	52
Illness and Healthcare	56
Guardians and Officers	68
Out-Relief and Relieving Officers	69
Vagrants	73
Financing the Workhouse	76
Spiritual Matters	78
Sailors and Soldiers	79
The Elderly	81
Emigration	83
Libel Against the Master	84
A Model Workhouse?	86
PART THREE - 1900-1948	90
On the Edge of Change	90
Administration	93
Clothes	93
The Children	94
Work Inside the Workhouse	98
The Infirmary	102
The First World War	103
Removal Orders	106

Vagrants	107
Unusual Cases	109
The Regime is Softened	109
The Workhouse Becomes the Institution	111
AFTER WORD 1948-1990	116
The Building Becomes a Hospital	116
Appendices	119
Appendix 1 - List of Masters	119
Appendix 2 - Some lists of Board of Guardians	121
Appendix 3 - Chairmen of the Board of Guardians	124
Appendix 4 - The inmates in 1861 on census night	126
Appendix 5 - The records of the Milton Union Workhouse	130
Bibliography	131
Index	133

CONTENTS

Acknowledgements	4
Introduction	7
PART ONE	9
The setting up the Union Workhouse 1834-1835	9
The Riots	13
The Workhouse Building	18
PART TWO - 1835-1900	26
Admission and Discharge	27
Work Inside the Workhouse	31
Discipline in the Early Years	36
The School in the Workhouse	40
Bread and Cheese	52
Illness and Healthcare	56
Guardians and Officers	68
Out-Relief and Relieving Officers	69
Vagrants	73
Financing the Workhouse	76
Spiritual Matters	78
Sailors and Soldiers	79
The Elderly	81
Emigration	83
Libel Against the Master	84
A Model Workhouse?	86
PART THREE - 1900-1948	90
On the Edge of Change	90
Administration	93
Clothes	93
The Children	94
Work Inside the Workhouse	98
The Infirmary	102
The First World War	103
Removal Orders	106

Vagrants	107
Unusual Cases	109
The Regime is Softened	109
The Workhouse Becomes the Institution	111
AFTER WORD 1948-1990	116
The Building Becomes a Hospital	116
Appendices	119
Appendix 1 - List of Masters	119
Appendix 2 - Some lists of Board of Guardians	121
Appendix 3 - Chairmen of the Board of Guardians	124
Appendix 4 - The inmates in 1861 on census night	126
Appendix 5 - The records of the Milton Union Workhouse	130
Bibliography	131
Index	133

Introduction

The days of the workhouse are long gone yet the memory of the harsh treatment which the poor suffered in these institutions, and the stigma felt by those obliged to live in them lingers on in handed-down memories. Locally and in many other towns in England, the workhouse was known as 'the spike', because of the iron spikes along the tops of the walls, and older people in Milton still recall how their own parents in old age pleaded with them not to let them end their days in the spike. Others have told me that, when they were children, they too had a fear of the place, because they had been threatened with 'ending up down the spike' if they did not behave themselves.

The poor of a large area of north east Kent went into the Milton Union workhouse which stood on the edge of the town of Milton Regis, in an unhealthy spot, low-lying by the creek of the Swale and with a stream running through the grounds in front of the building.

The creek was at the heart of Milton and was alive with smacks, hoys and sailing barges casting off daily from its wharves for London. They carried bricks and paper made in the town, as well as the apples and cherries from the orchards in the neighbouring villages. Ash from London refuse tips was loaded onto the barges on their return to be used in brick making. Passengers also embarked on the regular hoys for London. Milton was a small industrial town and cargo port with ancient oyster fisheries which declined during the Victorian period. Throughout the existence of the Milton Union there were thriving brick fields around the town.

Milton adjoins Sittingbourne which was then another small town which had made its name by being a stopping place for stagecoach travellers between London and Dover on Watling Street. The remainder of the Milton Union area was then agricultural, and the inhabitants of the villages were largely farm workers.

During its first fifty years the regime for the inmates of the new workhouse was harsh and the living conditions poor. Then, from the 1880s onwards, came gradual improvement and a greater interest in the institution began to be taken by the community.

Eventually the workhouse was taken over by the newly created National Health Service as a hospital for the elderly. It finally closed in 1990, 155 years after the building opened, and was demolished in the early 1990s when flats were built on the site. Nothing now remains to remind the passer by of what was for so long an intimidating part of the local scene.

PART ONE

The setting up the Union Workhouse 1834-1835

In 1835 a large and forbidding two storey building was built in North Street Milton Regis to house some of the poorest inhabitants of eighteen largely rural parishes which had been formed into a group or union. The parishes were Bapchild, Bobbing, Borden, Bredgar, Hartlip, Iwade, Kingsdown, Lower Halstow, Milstead, Milton Regis, Murston, Newington, Rainham, Rodmersham, Sittingbourne, Tong, Tunstall and Upchurch. The joint population of these parishes was then just 10,700 of which the vast majority lived in Sittingbourne and Milton, the two adjacent towns. The passing of the Poor Law Amendment Act of 1834 meant that parishes had to group together to build joint workhouses for their poor and so substantial workhouse buildings began to go up all over the country.

Poverty in the early 19th century was caused not only by unemployment, but also by wages so low that farm workers in the south-east of England could not maintain their families. Thus the farmers, some of whom were wealthy, were paying inadequate wages. Most of the poor in the Milton Union area were farm workers who were employed by the job or by the day, instead of by the year as they had been in the past. Added to this difficulty was the lack of any sickness benefit or old age pension.

The idea of workhouses was not a new one. Each parish had long been responsible for its own poor and some were housed in small workhouses established in the 18th century, whilst most were given out-relief. Out-relief meant helping to maintain the poor in their own homes by giving them food, money or clothes. This out-relief would be given to the sick, the out of work, and also to those whose wages were thought to be below subsistence level for a family. Help would sometimes be given with other needs such as the cost of the village midwife, a blanket or some coal. Before the 1834 Act, the churchwardens and overseers of every parish raised their own rates to relieve the poor and organised their relief within the parish. Poor rates had been rising steadily since the end of the eighteenth century and some rate payers felt that there were many amongst the poor who would rather be supported by them than work for a living. They saw the parish system as ripe for change.

We must not suppose that conditions in parish workhouses had necessarily been any better than in the large union workhouses which followed them. The inmates of the Milton parish workhouse had not been free to come and go as they pleased on a daily basis, they had to have permission from the Master or Matron and indeed at times were confined to the house as a punishment and only fed bread, cheese and water. A uniform was introduced in the Milton parish workhouse in 1832 and furthermore 'all young single men shall be kept in the workhouse and not suffered to go out and to be fed on bread and cheese except on Sunday and then they are to go to church.'[1]

Milton was a large workhouse and conditions in the smaller village workhouses were usually less regimented and in some cases quite comfortable. Parish workhouses did have two advantages over the large union houses

---

[1] CKS P253 / 8 / 4

which followed them: they were small and so everything was on a personal scale, and the inmates were close to home with people they knew.

The 1834 Act aimed to stop all out-relief to the able-bodied on the principle that if they were fit they should be able to maintain themselves and if they could not then they must enter the workhouse. Upon arrival they would be separated from their families and given back-breaking work to do. The new workhouses were to act as a deterrent; a warning to those whom the gentry and farmers saw as the undeserving poor. The act also had the opposing aim of providing a place of refuge for the sick and the disabled. The two aims were to prove difficult to achieve together.

Poor Law Commissioners were appointed for each area of the country to help to organise the new unions and building works. Sir Francis Bond Head became the Assistant Commissioner for Kent, which suited him well since his family were from the county. He was an energetic, decisive, military man in the prime of life, who had served with the Royal Engineers, been present at Waterloo, and in more recent years managed a mining company in South America. In his new role he travelled all over Kent, living up to his nick-name of 'Galloping Head,' inspecting existing workhouses and forming new unions. His opinion was that many of the larger old parish workhouses were too comfortable, the food too good making them attractive to the poor. No such laxity would exist under the new regime. By July 1835 he had formed eleven east Kent unions.

The first meeting for the setting up of the Milton Union workhouse was held at the old parish workhouse in Milton on March 11th 1835. Sir Francis was there and representatives of the eighteen local parishes who had been elected to the Board of Guardians by the ratepayers. Guardians were usually farmers, small business-men and shopkeepers.

This map shows the Milton Union area and its eighteen parishes as follows:1. Rainham, 2. Upchurch, 3. Hartlip, 4. Lower Halstow, 5. Newington, 6. Iwade, 7. Bobbing, 8. Borden, 9. Bredgar, 10. Milton, 11. Sittingbourne, 12. Tunstall, 13. Milstead, 14. Kingsdown, 15. Rodmersham, 16. Bapchild, 17. Murston, 18. Tonge.

The Rev. Dr. Poore, magistrate of Murston was elected chairman and Sir John Tylden vice-chairman. Sir Francis read his speech explaining the duties of the new board. He reassured them that they would be 'shielded and protected and supported by the Power of the Central Poor Law Board' and that 'in no one instance will you be called upon to refuse Relief, without having it in your Power to shew the Applicant....the very clause in the

Act....which strictly forbid you to comply with their request.'

Sir Francis was aware that the idea of the new workhouse was unpopular but, he went on 'when it is fully understood how capable you are of elevating the character of the Kentish labourer....your....situation.... will be highly respected.' Presumably he envisaged the respect coming from other rate payers rather than the poor.

The Riots

Before the new workhouse was built the Milton Guardians decided to press ahead with the implementation of the changes in out-relief required by the new act. This meant that the amount of money paid in out-relief to the able bodied who were out of work and being made to do tasks for the parish, would be cut, and the remainder made up with a voucher for bread. The farm labourers were quick to express their anger with the change. They had been through years of poor wages and difficulty in finding work. There was similar unrest in the neighbouring Faversham union area. On the 3rd of May the Rev. Poore, Rector of Murston (and veteran of the 1830 labourers' riots in the district) wrote to the Home Secretary, Lord John Russell, of the difficulties in the area:

> *In consequence of great excitement created in this Neighbourhood by attempting to carry the new Poor Law Bill into execution Sir Samuel Chambers and myself found it our duty....to swear in yesterday at Bredgar where the poor were about to be relieved, three special*

> constables for three months. Sir Samuel resides in the parish but from the infirmities of age is unable to take a very active part. I continued there in the room with the relieving officer for the first hour or two and I believe had not these precautions been taken there would have been a serious riot.[2]
>
> On the preceding Thursday at Bapchild the same relieving officer and an overseer were forcibly expelled by the poor from the room and their papers and books torn to pieces but with the exception of a few bruises they received no personal injury.
>
> I am just informed by the clerk of our division that it is <u>rumoured </u>that a large assemblage of persons from Newnham, Lenham and Neighbourhood is to take place at Doddington tomorrow to obstruct the relieving officer…[3]

Three days later Sir Francis Head wrote from Sittingbourne to the Poor Law Commissioners with further grave news:

> 'I attended the weekly meeting of the Guardians of the Milton Union – they are determined to resist any intimidation and will go with their relieving officers to their respective parishes….the terms which the insurgents demand are impossible for they insist on receiving relief <u>entirely in money</u> their object being to spend that money at the beer shop. This they call <u>their rights</u> ….Dr. Poore was forcibly detained at Doddington by the

---

[2] See The agricultural riots of 1830 in the Sittingbourne area by Helen Allinson, Bygone Kent, vol 3 no. 46

[3] NA MH12 / 5279

> *mob, actually assaulted, and he even had a personal struggle with one of the gang... A number of the peasantry armed with sticks have assembled today in various directions and a crowd of them, surrounding us during our meeting at the Milton Workhouse...they followed us tolerably peacefully for about half a mile, they then began to pelt us with stones of which the Guardians took no notice until it was found necessary to turn our horses heads and canter towards them- this completely stopped everything not another stone was thrown.*
> *I have printed handbills and say I will meet the people at Greenstreet next Friday.'*

The handbills read : 'Having heard that considerable numbers of the labouring classes are tumultuously assembling in various places to obstruct the relieving officers Sir Francis Head will meet them at Greenstreet next Friday.' Head obviously had faith in his own ability to calm the crowds and felt that calling in the military would escalate matters.

Sir Francis continued,

> *'at present we want no support whatever but I hope you will be pleased to use your influence with the Archbishop of Canterbury to prevail on Dr Poore to return his commission of the peace....it is not only my opinion that he is implacably hostile to the Poor Law Amendment Act. It is very painful to me to make this application to you....now....it should be concealed from Dr. Poore....to whom I have no animosity and from whom I have received many acts of personal enmity.'*

Naturally Dr. Poore and Sir Francis had very different views of the situation. The one a local clergyman, the other a military man. Sir Francis had hoped to get Dr. Poore on his side by appointing him chairman of the Guardians but he had almost immediately resigned, though he continued to attend meetings as one of the board.[4]

Frankly Sir Francis had alarmed the establishment with his idea of a big meeting of labourers. The Poor Law Commissioners hastened to write that they hoped he would not go ahead with it on the 8th March. They had heard from the Lord Lieutenant of the county, the Marquis of Camden, who also deplored the idea. Sir John Tylden the new chairman of the Milton Union Guardians also wrote at length to the Commissioners. He, however was happy with Sir Francis's ideas and also put his view that a permanent rural police force would be useful.

The Milton Guardians gave long and detailed written instructions to their hapless relieving officers who were now in the unenviable position of implementing the new act. Relieving officers assessed applications for relief and distributed out-relief. They were not to be too severe but were to act with kindness and humanity yet firmness and determination particularly with 'depraved characters'. So quite a balancing act was required! Out-relief in kind would mainly be bread 'but where the character is good, part may be in bacon.' They were to listen patiently to complaints and to act with humanity in cases of distress. The distinction being made between the deserving and undeserving poor was one which was to last and last. All this was too much for one of the relieving officers, John Vinton, who resigned in May due to the violence he

---

[4] for an excellent account of the riots see Money or Blood, D. Hopker (1988)

encountered.[5] The Guardians then straight way resolved that if the conduct of the paupers was too violent then the relieving officer could tell them that they must come to the workhouse to receive their relief there at a given time.[6]

On the 4th May Dr. Poore wrote from Murston with news of troubling events at Doddington. 'On our arrival we found 200 or more armed with bludgeons, many of them were strangers and were saying, 'We will have money only!' Sir John Tylden was present at Rodmersham on the 7th when the relieving officer for the first time gave only half the out-relief in money and the remainder as a ticket for bread. The crowd gathered at the church became frenzied, the military were called in and arrests made[7].

The Milton Guardians agreed to go out to the villages with their relieving officers to ensure order when relief was given. The original aim of giving able-bodied men their relief in tickets only was put off until the new workhouse was ready for occupation.

On May 19th the 'Maidstone Gazette' reported riots in the area. The labourers 'assembled in considerable numbers, and demanded relief to be given to them in money. Failing in their demands, several acts of violence were committed, such as the breaking of windows.' The report went on to state that several ringleaders were taken before the Rev. Poore, who in his capacity as magistrate released them when they promised good conduct. However this was by no means the end of the matter. Trouble increased and soldiers were sent for from

---

[5] CKS G/Mi AM1
[6] ibid
[7] ibid

Chatham. The labourers assembled in large numbers and for a while they had Rev. Poore locked into the Rose Inn in Sittingbourne High Street. It was found necessary for the soldiers to form ranks.

> 'The officer in command immediately ordered his men to fix bayonets and load with ball cartridge. This being done, he informed Dr. Poore that he awaited his orders to fire. Immediately the malcontents heard this they separated in all directions, and being pursued between twenty and thirty were taken into custody.'

The report concludes dryly: 'The New Poor Law is certainly anything but popular here.' The disturbances were however short-lived and unorchestrated and the Milton Union Board were soon able to continue with the business of setting up the new workhouse.

The Workhouse Building

Three of the new Guardians, Sir John Tylden, William Gascoyne of Bapchild, and Edward Homewood of Tunstall, were appointed to inspect the existing Sittingbourne and Milton workhouses within their union area and decide whether they could be used to meet the requirements of the act. Clearly they did not waste time in looking at the workhouses of the villages in the union since none were large enough to be of use for their purposes. They produced a full and thoughtful report which was accepted by the rest of the Guardians.[8]

---

[8] CKS G/MiAM1

The committee decided that the poor should be divided into three categories as they had been instructed:
1. The Aged and Infirm both married and single.
2. The younger married people having families and without. The younger single women and the children.
3. The able-bodied single men and ill conducted Refractory married Men.

Each category they planned to put in a separate building as recommended by the act. The elderly and sick were to go in the old Milton workhouse, the able-bodied single males in the new one and married couples and children in the old Sittingbourne workhouse. Although the Guardians intended to put children in the same building as their parents, parents were not to eat or sleep near them nor have any control over them. In their aim of putting young married couples together they showed more compassion than the Commissioners, and they felt it necessary to justify themselves.

> 'We consider that, except as a punishment for bad conduct, husband and wife ought not to be separated, for altho' the great object is to render Pauperism as distasteful as possible to the lower class, still poverty may not be a Crime.'

In spite of this intention, once the new workhouse was open married couples did not have separate rooms and were not able to stay together. This was the case throughout England. The Guardians accepted that families whose conduct was good and 'who do not deserve to be treated with any unnecessary harshness'[9] would be admitted to the workhouse.

---

[9] ibid

The intentions of the committee towards the elderly were very good; they recognised that the old had a 'strong prejudice against going into the House', and suggested using old Milton parish workhouse for the aged and the ill and naming it 'The Alms house' and 'we would endeavour to make their old age as comfortable and happy as we can do consistent with that economy so absolutely necessary'. It was felt that there was also room for part of the old Milton workhouse to be the hospital for the union and that 'nurses would be easily selected from the old people on the spot.' Since the garden of the workhouse was extensive the committee thought there was plenty of room to erect a new building for the able-bodied men large enough to contain 500. The Sittingbourne parish workhouse in the High Street was considered suitable for about 100 children and up to 40 single women, then some building could be added in the yard for the married couples. They supposed that one of the dining halls could be a school room and there was also room for a workshop for the children who 'ought to be taught as many useful trades as possible.'

The committee was impressed by the cleanliness, neatness and order of the Milton and Sittingbourne workhouses and therefore recommended that the Master and Matron of both should be kept on, but in the event there were jobs only for one couple. The Aldertons who ran the Milton workhouse were appointed. Oliver Alderton was to be paid £80 a year plus food and accommodation, jointly with his wife Elizabeth as Matron. However they were to find themselves out of their depth in the large new institution.

The plans to keep the two old workhouses and build a third might perhaps have been preferable for the inmates than all living together in the new building. After accepting the report the Board added two men to the committee; William Fairman and William Bland, in order to move matters forward on the new building for able-bodied men. The augmented committee looked at the site and found the garden of the existing workhouse too small for their purposes and recommended the purchase of the adjoining small field. There would be a part of this left which could be a garden for the portion of the old workhouse which was to be converted to a hospital. The low thatched building then used as a coal shed and dining room in the existing workhouse was what they had in mind for the hospital which could be converted at a 'very trifling expense.'

The land was purchased for £42 to enable building the new workhouse next to the old one at Milton. Meanwhile the guardians continued to hold their meetings in the old Milton workhouse. Building costs were not to exceed £4000 and a loan was taken out for this sum.

Although the Guardians had asked William Bland to draw up a plan for the new workhouse and he had done so, it was in the event the design of Sir Francis Head himself which they used. Head's ideal was that of a prison-like building with blind outer walls and a courtyard within. His ideas were accepted by twelve unions in Kent, but outside his personal sphere of influence none chose his design in spite of its appealing cheapness to build.[10] Most workhouses in England were more attractive in design and perhaps most were also a little better to live in. Many were larger and contained hundreds more inmates, but few could have presented

---

[10] The Workhouse: A study of poor-law buildings in England. Kathryn Morrison (English Heritage 1999)

such a grim face to the passer by. The building was superintended by William Bland.

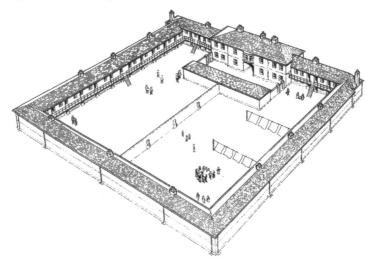

View of Sir Francis Head's design for a rural workhouse to accommodate 500 people. The design was used with minor modifications by 12 Kent unions. The yard was divided by extra walls to separate the different categories of inmates. The blank outer walls can clearly be seen. (Reproduced with the permission of English Heritage NMR)

Sir Francis's design meant that all the first floor dormitories were entered from a narrow iron gallery reached by external stairs. How unpleasant this must have been in winter, and then there was the fact that all windows faced inwards onto the courtyard so that no glimpse of life in the world outside could be seen. Most of the workhouses of the Sir Francis Head design did not have internal staircases built or the galleries removed until late in the nineteenth century. No windows, other than in the infirmary, were placed in the outer walls until 1867.

Living accommodation took up most of three sides of the building and on the fourth were the Master's quarters, the board room, the clerk's office, the entrance archway, kitchen and washhouse.

The many small dormitories were spartan, furnished with iron bedsteads and mattresses filled with straw. Each dormitory slept eight and was only fifteen feet by ten feet, with one window, so each individual had very little space. More double bedsteads than single were purchased by the Guardians and the inmates were expected to share. This was common practice in the early years of the unions. The mattresses were stuffed with oaten chaff and oaten straw cut. The windows on the ground floor were overshadowed by the iron galleries above, extra ventilation was provided by cast iron gratings in the courtyard walls. The courtyard was unpaved until 1842 and therefore muddy in winter. It was divided by walls twelve feet high to keep the men and women out of each others sight when they were outside for exercise. An enclosed stable with space for fourteen horses was rapidly provided for the Guardians some of whom had to ride a number of miles from their parishes.

The building was lit with candles and lamps, though in 1852 gas lighting was installed in some of the rooms.

There was the absolute minimum of sanitation, for each side of the building had a single unlit privy, upstairs and downstairs, so each catered for about a hundred people, though seventy-two chamber pots were bought. The smell would have been unspeakable, and the risk to health great. Water was pumped from a well in the yard. Extra privies were added in 1845, but it was to be many years before there was much improvement in the sanitary arrangements. At the corners of the building lay the dayrooms and workrooms.

It was quickly found that all categories of the poor could be accommodated in the one new workhouse at Milton, and the plans for using the other two were dropped.

At the end of the Guardians first year in office, in April 1836, Sir John Tylden made a long, congratulatory speech to his fellow Guardians reminding them of all the progress they had made, the personal danger they had been in at the start, the prompt putting down of the riot, and the labourers improved conduct. He said

> *'they at once altered their conduct and manner: and we can all now bear testament to the improved habits and bearing of our Labourers. Indeed if we consider how the Old system of Poor Law had been gradually teaching the lower classes that they had a <u>right</u> to be supported by the Higher, the moment temporary causes threw them out of work, or as in too many cases they were too idle to seek for work.'*[11]

He felt that their two purposes had been achieved; the cutting of the poor rate and the improved habits of the poor. People of Sir John's class wished to see the poor sober, industrious and moral in their habits.

At first it had been thought that 2000 paupers would be housed in three workhouses but now all were in the one new building and it was not full. The harsh institutional regime of the workhouse made it extremely unpopular with the poor so that just as intended, none came in who could possibly avoid it. The average annual total of

---

[11] CKS G/MiAM1

money spent on the poor in the union for the three years ending 1835 had been £11,197. Now it was £5,638. Half of those who had been on relief in the union area were so no longer. People had been driven away by the harsh terms and conditions. Circumstances would dictate that spending gradually increased again in the years to come.

PART TWO - 1835-1900

During its first seven years the Milton Union workhouse was run badly as we shall see, by a couple with none of the necessary characteristics to make for a smoothly running institution. For three of these years the situation for the children of the workhouse was dreadful as they were in the hands of a pair of corrupt and cruel teachers. After 1842 with the appointment of a new Master and Matron, the Cobbolds, matters gradually improved for the inmates. Despite the rigid framework of the Poor Law Act, conditions varied from one workhouse to another depending upon the attitudes and abilities of the Master and Matron and the efficiency and kindness of the Guardians. Yet the over all feeling remained that the poor everywhere were being punished for their poverty.

To begin with the Guardians struggled to understand all of the many rules and regulations of the act under which they operated, so that when one of the Poor Law Commissioners visited Milton in 1836 they had a variety of questions to ask. The first two concerned those on out-relief. Could clothes be given to the child of an able-bodied man when he or she was going out into service as had been customary? They could not. Could the cost of a midwife be allowed, for an able-bodied labourers wife? It could not. In the case of large families could part of the family go into the workhouse? They could not. Could the old inmates go out for air and exercise? Certainly not, was the Commissioners reply.[12]

---

[12] ibid

So we have to bear in mind that sometimes when the Guardians appeared to take very harsh actions they were following the letter of the law. But on another occasion the question they raised was whether they had to clothe illegitimate babies when they left the workhouse. This clearly went against the grain. The Guardians feeling was that these girls who got into trouble should find their babies' clothes themselves. Shockingly, as a result, two babies had left the workhouse naked[13] and this showed that the Milton Guardians were indeed a flinty group of men, verging on the inhumane. From their own narrow perspective they would have said they were making sure not to encourage permissive behaviour.

Admission and Discharge

The destitute people who saw no other way to survive than to enter the workhouse could make their way to Milton and appear at the weekly meeting of the Board of Guardians to request admittance, or they could apply to the relieving officer who came to their parish. If taken in they were brought to a receiving ward where they were stripped, bathed, treated with flea and bug powder, and issued with uniform. For the boys there were short frocks (smocks), and canvas trousers and boots. Their own clothes were taken to be washed and stored. They were then separated husband from wife, parents from children. The following day they would be examined by the medical officer who decided whether they would be classified as able-bodied or sick and then they were taken to the appropriate ward.

---

[13] CKS G/MiAM1

The reasons given for admission (in the admission and discharge books), show why some of the poor had no choice but to go in to the hated workhouse when they fell on hard-times. Unemployment or low wages, illness or widowhood, or age combined with infirmity were the most common causes. Less frequently there were children who had been deserted or who were orphans, and mothers who had been deserted by their husbands who could not earn enough to feed their children. Girls who had been turned out by their families because they were pregnant had 'having a bastard' written beside their name in the admission book. Poor Susan Dean was one of these women and she sadly died in giving birth in 1839. George and John Black were Sittingbourne orphans who had no choice but to turn to the workhouse in 1840 when they were just too young to make their own way in the world.

If a man was sent to prison or transported, his family often ended up in the workhouse as was the case with Hannah Eason of Milton who came in with her four children in 1839. Mary Twirl of Newington was another such case for her husband was transported and she had to be admitted with her three children.

Then there were always many vagrants who wandered from workhouse to workhouse. Many families whose bread-winner was intermittently out of work, would go in and out of the workhouse many, many times, leaving as soon as they had a chance of work. Others such as the frail elderly, once admitted, were likely to remain for the rest of their lives. Some of these kept trying to manage outside, such a one was Richard Rossiter of Milton an eighty year old widower who had been a 'showman', with a fair no doubt. Another was William Webb a Milton waterman too old and unwell to find employment by 1840.

Some people so disliked the workhouse life that they preferred to risk starvation. Seventy year old James Featherstone of Bredgar made this decision in December 1840 when he left Milton workhouse and set off to try and scrape a living by selling matches. He walked on through his own village and was discovered frozen to death on the top of Hollingbourne Hill, an embarrassment to the Guardians of the Hollingbourne union.[14]

After the first year or two, there was a decline in the number of illegitimate children admitted which was a matter for self-congratulation for the Guardians. This decline was due to the fact that mothers could no longer leave their child in the workhouse while they supported themselves, but had to enter with the child. The explanation of the Guardians was different -'the crime of bastardy was decreasing and many illegitimate children formerly supported by the parish are now supported by their relations', they said.

The number of able-bodied men in the workhouse declined during the 1840s (as in workhouses generally) for there was more work to be had. By 1849 only a handful of able-bodied men were inmates at Milton and this situation was repeated all over the country.

In later years the interviews for admittance were reported in the local press. So in April 1881

'A woman attended the meeting and asked the board to allow her husband's mother to be admitted to the house. She was infirm and quite helpless and the applicant, having a family and

---

[14] NA MH 12 5136

> *being a delicate woman herself, felt wholly unequal to the task of attending to her. Her husband would be willing to contribute towards the maintenance of his mother in the workhouse.'*

Two Guardians felt she should be admitted but the rest felt that though the case was a hard one,

> *'they must set their faces against the practice of persons seeking to put relatives into the workhouse who were a burden to them, thus shifting the responsibilities from their own shoulders on to the shoulders of the ratepayers, and that they must adhere to the principle of making the workhouse what it was intended to be, a place for the relief of destitution and not a lodging house.'*[15]

This principle of not running a lodging house, was a favourite one for the board, and was equally applied that year to the case of a working man whose wife had died and who wanted to pay for his children to be maintained in the workhouse. He too was turned away.

An eleven year old boy arrived alone at the gates in November 1880. His name was Henry Court and he had left his sister's house in Canterbury and walked, thinking he was making his way to another sister at East Grinstead. He had slept under the hedges. He was granted admittance and enquiries were made about him.

How did the inmates get discharged from the workhouse? Some were released only by death or if they recovered from illness they were signed off by the medical officer. The most frequent reason given in the

---

[15] East Kent Gazette April 23 1881

admission and discharge books is 'discharged at own request', which meant that inmates applied to the Guardians via the Master for discharge to seek work. If they also requested out-relief then they were often told to remain inside. A few inmates in the early years were discharged into prison for bad conduct in the workhouse. James Moon a young unemployed labourer from Tong was taken before the magistrate and given a 21 day sentence for scaling the building, wearing union clothes and being absent all night. The clerk recorded a comment about the conduct of the inmate in the admission and discharge book, usually it was simply 'good or 'very good' but it could be 'poor' or 'disobedient'.

Although the majority of the male inmates were farm workers, there were always a considerable group in Milton who were mariners, fishermen or sailors and another group who were brick field labourers. For example the 1881 census shows seven men whose previous work had been at sea, and twelve who had worked on the near by brick fields.

Between 1841 and 1901, the number of inmates reflected the local economic situation and availability of work. So in 1841 there were 235 inmates, the 1851 census showed only 115, the 1861 census just 87. There were 142 in 1871, 131 in 1881 and in 1901 there were as many as 283. These totals can be read as a barometer of local economic prosperity, recording as they do, the rising and falling of local unemployment and the consequent social distress.

Work Inside the Workhouse

Within the workhouse the aim was to provide a disciplined regime of grinding monotony which no one could prefer to struggling with poverty at home. Once admitted within the walls, a strict timetable was adhered to, so that in summer the paupers had to rise at 5am (a time which they would have been used to if they had worked on the land). Breakfast was between six and seven, then for the able-bodied there was work until 12. Work continued from one until five. Supper was then served and the inmates were obliged to go to bed at eight. In winter the inmates rose at seven, had breakfast between seven-thirty and eight whilst the rest of the day the timetable was the same all year round.

The able-bodied were given hard and monotonous work to do, which for the women included cleaning the workhouse and doing all the cooking, sewing and washing. The women made most of the uniforms under the guidance of Matron. Lucy Cobbold who became Matron in 1842, was so zealous in this that she and her husband were rewarded with a rise in salary in thanks for all the money she had saved the board in clothing costs. Some women, perhaps those who were older, were given the more pleasant task of knitting worsted stockings for the inmates.

Oakum was bought in by the hundred-weight to be picked, in some unions such as Faversham this unpleasant job was only undertaken as a punishment but in the harsher regime at Milton it was routine. This was a painful task, for unravelling old ropes so that they could be used to provide fibre for packing between shrinking ships planks, made the fingers of the workers raw and liable to infection. The institution made little profit being paid a few shillings per hundred weight, but the advantage was in keeping the poor unpleasantly occupied. Men were required to pick 4lb of oakum a day and women three.

In December 1840 John Cook of Borden, appeared before the magistrates for refusing the task. It was equally a job done by the female paupers and sometimes they too refused, as when Mary Seager did in1841. Mary lacked control of her temper and within months was standing in front of the magistrate again, this time for 'the most violent language to the Master and two of the Guardians'[16] More often the poor found strength in numbers and several refused to work at a time, then all were brought before the magistrate for sentencing.

The theme of difficult work as punishment can still be seen years later when in 1879 the Guardians discussed the idea of a room specifically for the women to pick oakum, for the practice of making women do this had fallen into disuse here. Several Guardians felt that young women who came in to give birth to their babies came in too early, and could usefully do this work rather than the sewing that they were then given. They felt that oakum picking might even decrease the number of women coming in to the workhouse.

Stone was regularly purchased by the Board and the men had to set about the back-breaking task of making three bushels of stones pass through half inch sieves. Large quantities of Guernsey granite were ordered at a time and delivered by ship to the Creek. In 1890 it was 250 tons of Guernsey granite spalls, in earlier years local flints were bought for the purpose. The work was done in the open in the yard though a shed was added for protection from the weather after a few years. The Guardians employed a Superintendent of Labour who had to be 'competent to superintend the men engaged in stone-breaking, and

---

[16] CKS G/Mi AM2

wood-cutting'.[17] Sometimes the superintendent was the same man who made the shoes for the inmates or was a tailor who made the clothes and instructed inmates in these skills.

In the 1980s, evidence still remained that the men had been given the task of stone breaking for these two stone breakers stood in a corner of the garden of the workhouse (by then a hospital). They had been used to pound large stones for road building, they are now kept by the Sittingbourne Society at Periwinkle Mill, Milton. (B. Allinson)

In 1842 the Guardians considered the idea of hiring some land for the able-bodied paupers and older children to work on, and with the sanction of the Commissioners, mattocks, spades and shovels were purchased, land rented, and work begun. The able-bodied were to dig two

---

[17] East Kent Gazette Jan 8 1881

perches (which was 5 ½ square yards), of the pasture land and ten perches of the arable land a day. An overseer was appointed to keep the workers on task and after a while the Guardians thought it best to provide a basic toilet in the field for the workers use. The land was directly opposite the workhouse, later a barn was erected there to store vegetables.

The elderly male inmates of the workhouse were involved in digging up potatoes and in 1843 the Guardians agreed that they should be allowed half an ounce of tobacco each in recognition of their efforts. After a few years the cultivation of the land fell largely to the old men and older boys as there were few able-bodied male inmates.

For a while the flints on this land were dug up and sold too. The Guardians bought an acre of this land in 1873, then ten years later they were able to purchase the whole of Acremans Field, as the land was called. In 1890 part of it was leased to George Gransden for brick earth excavation and then flints. Three years later the brick makers, Wills and Packham, were allowed to lay a pipe for the carriage of brick making slurry through the edge of the workhouse garden. Then they requested a portion of the garden for a tramway to carry bricks and this was also accepted in return for a piece of land on the other side of the stream.[18]

In 1892 a tender was put out for three freights of best London manure, which was three 90 ton barge loads, to be delivered to the workhouse field.[19] So the field still used for growing vegetables must have been beside the field rented out for brick earth.

---

[18] CKS G/MiAM18

[19] CKS G/MiAM17

In some years wood was also chopped up and put into bundles to be sold. Over 53,000 such bundles were assembled in the first half of 1881.[20] At other times mats and netting were also made and sold to boost the union funds.

Discipline in the Early Years

Once admitted the inmates of the workhouse were far from free to come and go as they pleased as this harshly restrictive resolution of 1835 shows:

> *'No pauper to leave the house without the Master considers he has reasonable grounds. Old inmates not allowed liberty of going out for air or exercise. No friend of any of the children to take them out of the house for any temporary purpose.'*

Visiting by most friends and relatives was in any case impossible because of the large area covered by the union which meant that some of the inmates were a long way from home.

In many ways life in the workhouse with its disciplined regime was like being in prison. Upon admission the inmates were issued with a uniform set of clothes; a reminder to the wearers of their dependant situation. Several times uniforms were considered to be stolen as when James Thomas scaled the walls in the night and ran off wearing the workhouse clothes. In fact there would have been no choice for him but to go in the clothes he was wearing. For the same offence young James

---

[20] East Kent Gazette, April 23 1881

Lippingwell of Bredgar was sentenced to three months in gaol.

The inmates knew the rules and if they broke them they could be taken before a magistrate. There were numerous instances of this at Milton during the 1840s. In 1841, 23 year old Mrs Susan Head, of Bredgar, appeared before the magistrate for disorderly conduct in the workhouse and threatening to strike the Master. Mrs Head was not a woman to take orders easily and a few months later she again appeared before the magistrate, this time for refusing to pick oakum. Nor was this to be her last appearance in court.

It was in 1841 that the Master checked with the Board that he had the power to confine an able-bodied pauper for refusing to work and they confirmed that he had. No doubt they believed it would save some trips to court.

This power had, already occasionally been used in the case of children. An entry from the minute book tells us that in December 1839 the Master resolved 'that Elizabeth Vant be punished by being confined in the Black Hole for twenty four hours for making use of very indecent language in the chapel on Sunday last and that her diet be altered for three days to bread and water only.' This is all the more shocking to read when it is known that Elizabeth from Lower Halstow was an eleven years old orphan and that the Black Hole was a coal hole. Elizabeth's stay in the workhouse was a long one and her behaviour did not improve with her years for in 1842 we find that she was still being punished for disorderly conduct. One of her offences in 1842 was that together with three other girls she 'wilfully and mischievously spoiled and destroyed Chamber Utensils' (chamber pots) for which they were all brought before the magistrate. It comes as no surprise to find a warrant issued against her a year later for stealing a workhouse shirt.

Five women were placed in the Black Hole in December 1841 as a punishment for their unruly behaviour and given only dry bread and water for the twenty-four hours they were kept there. Rebellion was in the air that week, for within days John Price, John Satteen, James White, William Weller, George Golding, Thomas Mitchell, James Satteen, and Daniel Welby were 'separately confined in an apartment provided for that purpose for twenty-four hours and kept on Bread and Water for refusing to attend divine service in the Union chapel on Sunday.'[21] Not all workhouses had designated rooms or cellars as lock-ups but both Thanet and Chatham did have their own 'black holes'.[22]

Of course this imprisonment in a room could only work if the inmates entered the room reasonably willingly when taken there by the Master and the porter. But if they refused, as happened a year later in the case of four men, then they had to be taken before the magistrate and could be given a short prison sentence.

There is no more mention of locking up inside the workhouse after the 1840s, the offenders were taken straight to the magistrate to be dealt with. In cases of minor infringements of the rules the inmates were admonished by the Master and then brought before the Board at their next meeting to have the message reinforced by the august chairman. In fact once the Cobbolds took over as Master and Matron in 1842 the number of offences decreased greatly for, unlike the

---

[21] CKS G/Mi AM2
[22] Religion and Society in Kent, 1640-1914, Yates, Hume & Hastings.

Aldertons, they were able to deal with the inmates in a calm and consistent manner.

Later in the 19th century public enquiries revealed that some workhouses were places of systematic cruelty and although Milton was not one of these yet the evidence shows that the regime there was particularly harsh under the Aldertons and when its records are compared with those of Hollingbourne it is clear that the Hollingbourne Union was run in a more compassionate way. There are no instances of inmates being locked up in the workhouse there at all. This is remarkable considering the rules and regulations which the Master and the Guardians had to comply with. It is not surprising to learn that there were plenty of other Kentish unions where assaults on the Master were common particularly in the early years of the system.

Boys had been known to make a run for freedom, so in 1840 the Milton Master ordered that an iron grating be fitted to their ward.[23] In fact inmates were not even allowed to speak to their friends outside, for when it was discovered in 1841 that some of the women were speaking to their friends in the street through the ventilation bricks, the building committee was asked 'to stop up such as they think necessary to prevent any communication with persons outside.'

The Guardians resorted to even more extreme methods by May 1841 when they instructed a Sittingbourne blacksmith to place spikes on the walls to prevent the paupers from getting in or out without permission. Even so Robert Wood managed to get out in 1842 leaving his four children in there chargeable to Sittingbourne rate

---

[23] CKS G /Mi AM2

payers. Spikes were added to the door between the yards in 1843 to make sure there was no mixing between the men and women.

In 1842 the Master was instructed to warn paupers 'who are of Bad Character and are constantly going in and out of the House' that they could not be admitted again the same day and this was soon amended to three days.

Late in the nineteenth century the discipline became less harsh for inmates other than the wandering vagrants who stayed briefly here.

The School in the Workhouse

For many years there was no relief from the grim surroundings of the institution for the children when they went to school, for they were taught within the workhouse. School attendance was not to become compulsory for another generation in England and so the young inmates were in general totally uneducated on entry.

During the first year of the union workhouse a proposal from the Poor Law Commissioners was considered, whereby they would decrease the number of orphaned or abandoned children in the institution by sending some of the older girls to Bakewell in Derbyshire, where there was a demand for labour. A list of girls aged between twelve and fifteen was drawn up and 'their immediate migration' discussed.[24] This idea of moving children around the country in order to make them economically viable falls on our modern ears like words from another

---

[24] CKS G/MiAM1

world, however this was an idea of the Poor Law Commissioners run in tandem with their support of emigration and mainly aimed at finding able-bodied men work in northern factories.

No more is heard of the idea in the minutes so perhaps it came to nothing, but it did give the Guardians the idea of sending a man to the north to discover if men could find work there. He was given a list of questions and £5, and as a result in January 1837 the Bredgar overseers were instructed to conduct William Elliott and his family to Paddington on their way to Derbyshire and clothing and £5 was given to them.[25]

There was a rapid turn-over of teachers in the early years which is unsurprising when the difficulty of their task is considered, faced as they were with a constantly changing population of pupils most of whom can never have been to school before. The teachers were poorly paid, untrained, and had to supervise the children all day until they went to bed. Lessons lasted a minimum of three hours a day but the children also had to work from a young age, helping with such tasks as cleaning and sewing. In these early years of the institution it was possible for children who were born in the workhouse or abandoned there to live inside for years without seeing the outside world.

It must have been a real treat for the older children when in 1855 George Smeed the local brick maker and landowner, and often a Guardian himself, asked the board for permission to let the children go hop picking on his farms. There is no mention of any payment in the minutes of the Guardians and one wonders whether they

---

[25] ibid

simply agreed as a favour to the man who was then arguably the most influential single individual in Sittingbourne and Milton. At any rate the children were collected and delivered daily in one of Smeed's carts, accompanied by the schoolmaster and mistress, but after a couple of weeks the Guardians were obliged to write to him complaining that they had been informed that 'the carts conveying the children to his hop grounds were in the habit of stopping at public houses and other persons get in with the girls'.[26] He was requested to make sure it did not happen again.

Neither teachers nor children had any entitlement to holidays. The teachers had to apply to the Guardians for days off and were occasionally allowed three days. Teaching standards within workhouses were generally appalling. In any case teaching the children to be literate was not considered as important as making them work and as they got older giving them some rudimentary training. In the case of the girls, this was for domestic service and for the boys in many workhouses it was tailoring or shoemaking. However the teachers were supposed to teach the children to read and write and the rudiments of the Christian religion. For some this was preparation for apprenticeships in other parts of the country; a convenient way to get them off the Guardians hands.

The first teachers at Milton were Richard Barnard and Jane Hobbs whose payment included accommodation in the workhouse, food, coal and candles. From their wages they were to provide books and all the other materials for the children to use - a big disincentive to buy much for their charges. However after a couple of years the

---

[26] CKS G / MilAM6

Guardians had realised that they needed to provide some materials themselves; worsted and needles were bought so that the girls could be taught to knit. The first teachers left after a year and their successors, a married couple, the Weatherheads, did rather better financially at £25 and £15 a year. They, too, were told to 'instruct the boys and girls in reading, writing and the principles of the Christian religion and such other instructions as are calculated to train them to habits of usefulness, industry and virtue - and to assist the Master and Matron (the Aldertons),in the performance of their duties and maintenance of order and due subordination in the workhouse.'[27] As we shall see about the only one of these aims to be fulfilled by the Whiteheads was inculcating subordination.

In 1839 the Weatherheads were sacked and straight away serious accusations were made against them. The only one to be recorded in the Guardians' minute book was that William Weatherhead[28] had been constantly drunk whilst working and that the Master had had to put the boys to bed as a result. It is true to say that in these early years of union workhouses those employed as teachers were sometimes drunks, illiterates or systematically cruel people.[29]

In fact as the records of the Poor Law Commissioners show[30], far more serious charges had been laid at Weatherhead's door, charges which the Guardians were anxious to keep quiet. The Rev. George Greaves, chaplain of the workhouse, wrote many detailed letters to the Commissioners detailing his worries and how all the

---

[27] ibid
[28] CKS G/Mi / AM2
[29] The Workhouse , Norman Longmate (1974)
[30] NA MH12 / 5280

Weatherheads' wrong doings had been covered up with the help of the Master whom he described as a 'compound of the booby and low trickster'.

The Rev. Greaves was able to show that Weatherhead had sexually abused several of the girls in his care. The lack of moral leadership given by the Master and the encouragement to immorality given by Weatherhead had led to a situation in which on occasion the older boys exposed themselves to one of the girls who 'called out obscenely from her room at night to the boys below'. This was one of several similar incidents reported by Greaves whom the children knew well from his regular visits. They had been too afraid to tell him what was going on while Weatherhead was still there although he had been able to see that the man was totally unfit to have children entrusted to his care. Rev. Greaves had been warned by the Master not to enter any criticisms in his official chaplain's book of visits.

In September 1839 Greaves received further evidence that a nine year old girl had been raped by Weatherhead. As well as writing to the Poor Law Commissioners and informing the Guardians, Greaves involved his fellow clergyman and local Justice of the Peace the Rev. Poore of Murston. Another girl, Elizabeth Vant stated that the porter had offered her money for intercourse. She told other girls that 'she was in the family way' and was removed to the women's ward. This accusation proved unfounded however and Greaves was informed that she had been moved because of her 'gross indecency'.[31]

After interviewing several girls the Rev. Poore wrote a report for the Poor Law Commissioners. He concluded

---

[31] ibid

that there was 'no probability of convicting Weatherhead' but 'no Doubt can exist of his having acted towards the children in a most abominable, indecent and criminal manner.' He continued 'I have not pressed charges against Weatherhead as I consider it impossible to convict him, and bringing so many children into court to be examined on such a charge without a moral certainty of conviction would be outraging public decency without advancing public justice.' He did add that he and the Guardians were anxious not to protect Weatherhead if there were any chance of proving his guilt.

Greaves wrote again to make the point that what the girl witnesses told Poore in a formal magisterial hearing was far less than they had told him, and went on to suggest that the girl thought to have been raped should be examined by a doctor to see if she was a virgin. The Commissioners' opinion was that the girls would be even less forthcoming before a jury, nor could they sanction a medical examination, so the case would not go forward.

The Guardians wrote to the Commissioners to say that they did not consider Greaves charges against Weatherhead proved. However they did bar Weatherhead from ever entering the workhouse again, whilst reproving Greaves for having gone above their heads to the Commissioners. They also made the point to him that 'we cannot refrain from stating that we consider great injury must arise to the morals of the children from repeated examination of such disgusting details as this day have been laid before the board.'[32]

In November Greaves brought further instances of the corrupting influence of the Weatherheads before the

---

[32] CKS G/MiAM1

Commissioners. 'The children of the workhouse were for a considerable time <u>systematically</u> taught to pilfer – more particularly by the infant mistress (Mrs Weatherhead) when they were out.' The determined way in which Greaves was pursuing the matter of the Weatherheads and the Master had made him some enemies amongst the Guardians, some of whom liked to think all was well and wanted no scandal, and he received a threatening letter from one of them.

By December 1839 he had decided he was fighting a lost cause and resigned. But this did not stop his letters to the Commissioners, and in March 1840 he wrote 'as I leave I must beg you will not allow yourselves by any representation, come from <u>whatever quarter it may</u> to be <u>deceived</u> into the opinion that the Aldertons are in any way qualified for the situations they occupy. They have neither principle, judgement nor intelligence.' One of the charges which Greaves laid against the Master was that he had put a woman whom he admitted he knew 'was of the worst description' (i.e. a prostitute) to help look after the girls. She remained there after Greaves complained, and she 'initiated several girls into revolting practices'. The Commissioners decided they would investigate the Master.

Upon the Weatherheads leaving, Mr and Mrs Griffin were appointed as teachers and they did try their best for the school and the children, but all the while that Alderton was still Master they were in a difficult situation. They stayed less than a year.

This photograph was taken from the courtyard in the 1980s when the building was a hospital. Part of one of the exterior staircases can just be seen on the right. (B. Allinson)

In 1842 the Guardians were dissatisfied with discipline in the institution and were considering whether the children would after all be better dealt with in a separate building as had originally been the plan. They thought of hiring or buying the old workhouse adjacent to the new one and housing the children there. To this end they surveyed the old workhouse to see what it would cost to make it suitable. At the same time they wrote to the Poor Law Commissioners enquiring whether there was any prospect of the children going to a School of Industry. The Commissioners replied that there was none whatsoever.[33] Schools of Industry were being built at the time and were boarding schools where children were taught rudimentary occupational skills such as tailoring, farming or shoemaking.

---

[33] CKS G / Mi AM3

Unsurprisingly, under the Aldertons the then teachers Mr Bellnett and Miss Jones were struggling with their task. Matters came to a head in November when all four were given a months notice to leave or resign,[34] and the idea of using the old workhouse was dropped. It is dismaying to find that Mr and Mrs Alderton were given a testimonial stating that the Board appreciated their moral, honest and correct conduct. The job had been unsuitable for them from the start and they were constantly drawn into confrontations with the inmates as can be seen from the number of cases of residents being abusive to the Master.

The Poor Law Commissioners wrote to enquire why the four were leaving and were told it was due to a great lack of discipline throughout the house.

After placing advertisements in The Times and holding interviews, John and Charlotte Reynolds from Gloucester were appointed as the new Master and Mistress of the house and William and Lucy Cobbold from Norfolk as the teachers. However when the Poor Law Commissioners heard of the new appointments they were unable to give their approval since the Reynolds had in fact been sacked from their previous post by order of the Commissioners. The Guardians instantly dismissed them; they had to leave the following morning. By this time they had been in charge of the workhouse for about a month. Their references were then sent to the Commissioners to show the Guardians justification in appointing them.

And so it came about that William Cobbold the teacher, and his wife Lucy found themselves unexpectedly appointed as Master and Matron of the workhouse. The

---

[34] ibid

Cobbolds were young, in their thirties, and their children came to live with them at the workhouse. With their installation a period of stability began; the Guardians had chosen well this time and the institution became calmer and more orderly in their charge.

After a short gap during which various inmates acted as teachers the grandly named Golding Newman Constable was appointed schoolmaster at £30 p.a. and Marianne Green schoolmistress at £20 p.a. with furnished rooms, double rations, coal, candles and soap. These appointments resulted in a minor controversy for the following week the Guardians resolved that 'no person who is a Dissenter be eligible to be schoolmaster or mistress'[35] and some felt that the appointments should be rescinded as neither were qualified according to the chaplain who had discovered they were not Anglicans. However their appointment was approved by the Commissioners and although Green only stayed two years, Newman Constable remained for seven before leaving to become Master of another workhouse. After 1846 it became more common for trained teachers to be employed in workhouses.

It was in 1842 that the Master was directed to provide the necessary tools for boys to learn a trade and for a while Stephen Chrisfield was employed to instruct the boys in shoemaking. Other trainers employed by the workhouse taught the boys tailoring and the girls domestic work to fit them for earning a living when they left.

Some orphaned boys who had lived in the institution for years were apprenticed to other trades when they became old enough to leave. Such a one was John Peters of

---

[35] ibid

Rainham who in 1844 was apprenticed to John Jordan to learn to be a dredger man until he was 21 when he would have 'the freedom of the Strood Oyster Fishery'.[36] John Lavender a poor boy from Lower Halstow was apprenticed in 1849 to George Smeed, one of the Guardians who had made his fortune from brick-making. George Smeed owned many barges and John was to serve on the 'George and Eliza' registered out of the neighbouring port of Faversham.

Another boy, Edward Croucher was sent to Ramsgate with a view to being apprenticed to the fishing trade in 1880 and wrote to the Guardians to state that he had given satisfaction on his first trip and that he should like to be bound. The process was then begun and entailed the Guardians' clerk going to Ramsgate to sign the documents in Edward's presence in front of a magistrate to show that he was bound of his own free will. This was particularly important in the case of boys who went to sea for they were liable to be called upon to serve their country in the navy if a war were declared. Edward was then given the customary new set of clothes.

Later he wrote touchingly[37] to say how much he missed the dog, which belonged to the Master, and asking how it was getting on, and that he would come to the workhouse on Christmas Day. This reminds us that for the children who had been brought up in the institution, it was their home and their family. In 1890 it was James Curtis aged fifteen who was bound apprentice to the sea service for four years to Charles Burley of Sittingbourne owner of the ship Fanny Rapson.[38]

---

[36] CKS G/MiAM3
[37] East Kent Gazette Nov 27 1880
[38] CKS G / MiAM 17

Poor Law Schools by now had their own inspectorate and in 1867 Thomas Holmes the boys' teacher was given a good report. In 1880 the East Kent Gazette recorded[39] the findings of the inspector after his visit to the workhouse school. 'He stated that the children passed fairly well in arithmetic, but were weak in reading and spelling, and their intelligence in Scripture was very poor. Needlework and the industrial training of the girls were well cared for.' One of the Guardians remarked on hearing this that 'children were constantly coming in and going out so that it was not surprising they knew very little; they had no time in which to learn.' This is fair comment.

In 1882 the Guardians wrote to the Local Government Board with a proposal that they should not appoint a new schoolmaster to replace the one who had just left but instead send the children to the Milton Board School and appoint an Industrial Trainer to teach the boys tailoring and act as a boys 'warder'. This was agreed[40] and so schooling in the workhouse came to an end and the children were enabled to see something of life outside it on a daily basis. In this decision as in several others the Milton Union lagged behind, for from the 1870s onwards increasing numbers of workhouses had sent their children to local schools.

No toys were provided in workhouses before 1890, so it is encouraging to note that the children had swings in 1881, which the Guardians considered excellent exercise.[41]

The experience of children in workhouses obviously varied and in areas where there were landed gentry

---

[39] East Kent Gazette Jan 31 1880
[40] CKS G/Mi / ACa
[41] East Kent Gazette Nov 1881

nearby they often interested themselves in the children and brought them gifts and invited them on outings. Hollingbourne Union is a good example of this where in the 1880s the children were invited to the local flower show and given fruit and books on a number of occasions. They were also all taken on a day trip to the Crystal Palace, an occasion which it would be hard to imagine occurring in Milton. The only treat we hear of in this period at Milton is the visit of Mrs Gascoyne of Bapchild Court at Christmas 1880 bringing oranges and nuts for the children.

Many children were born in the workhouse over the years, usually to unmarried mothers, for example during the 1870s only 5 of the 72 children born there were born to married women. Sometimes the records afford us haunting glimpses of individual tragedies as when Charlotte Carter died in the workhouse in 1850, aged 19, leaving a baby who was soon sent to the Faversham workhouse.

Bread and Cheese

The diet of workhouse inmates everywhere was to be plain and monotonous. The Poor Law Commissioners laid down a choice of six similar dietaries; that chosen at Milton meant that every day breakfast and supper would be 6oz bread with ½ oz cheese or sometimes butter. The main meal of the day was little different since on four days it consisted of bread and cheese, two days suet pudding and vegetables and one day meat pudding and vegetables. Water was the drink, although old people were allowed tea and milk as extras and children were permitted milk twice a day. For many, this diet, meagre though it sounds to us, was often better than they had been eating outside.

The oven discovered when clearing out what was then the sewing room of Milton hospital in 1990 - courtesy V. Seary.

The small amount of meat which the paupers were given consisted of cheap cuts of beef, buttocks, 'clods and stickings' which were parts of the neck or throat of cows and sheep. The staff did rather better, having joints bought for them. Initially the food was cooked by some of the female inmates under the supervision of Matron, but in 1844 the first cook was appointed and paid £10 a year. Clearly any desire to experiment with recipes would be a drawback in the job and strong muscles a necessity in view of the quantities involved.

Surprisingly knives and forks were not provided for the inmates, though spoons were and spittoons for the old men. However in 1842 the Guardians decided that the fact that some paupers had knives and forks which they brought with them whilst others had to eat with their fingers was causing arguments so they decided the porter should take away cutlery on admission and that it would be provided by the union. Pint and quart tins were provided as drinking utensils and 16 dozen wooden trenchers were bought as plates.

As early as 1839 concessions were made towards celebrating Christmas, and a 'special dinner' which was actually a normal Sunday dinner, was given to the inmates and this became the annual custom with the addition of plum pudding from quite early on.

The Master was instructed to provide apples for the children in 1841 with a view to making them healthier and the younger ones were given rice puddings, which after some years were topped with a little treacle.

Few old people had their teeth and many had difficulty chewing the bread, so in 1843 the old men wrote a petition to the Guardians[42] complaining about the food. This was discussed with the medical officer and then it was agreed that dinner on Mondays and Saturdays could be a pint and a half of pea soup with 4oz of bread, instead of bread and cheese. The elderly were also to be allowed much more tea, two pints daily each sweetened with sugar, nor was this all, for there was to be an additional meat pudding dinner on Thursday instead of bread and cheese. These changes met with the approval of the Poor Law Commissioners.

---

[42] CKS G/ Mi AM3

In March 1863 there came a red-letter day. The Prince of Wales married Princess Alexandra and the Guardians conceded that the inmates should have a share in the celebration by being provided with plum pudding, tobacco, ale and snuff. The children were permitted to join the town procession to the wool warehouse Benecke Brothers, for a sit down tea. The entrance to the workhouse was decorated with banners, flags and a crown made of evergreens.

Two elderly men boldly brought their complaints about the quality of the food to the board in 1865.[43] They told the Guardians that the soup was sour and not fit to eat and that there was no union in England where the food was worse. The chairman decided that the old men were not to be believed.

Over the years the diet changed little, but supper was changed to bread and butter rather than bread and cheese and breakfast had in fact declined to bread and gruel rather than bread and cheese. By the 1890s it was agreed that the children could be given 2oz of jam four times a week in lieu of butter and adults 2oz of jam with their suet pudding.

The sick were always provided with different food at the discretion of the medical officer and the Admission and Discharge books of the union lists those who were ill and the variations in diet they were to receive, such as 'John Cook half pint porter, Eliza Honey 1 pint of milk until weaned'; with concluding remarks in each case either 'discontinued' if they got better, or almost as frequently in the early years 'dead'. When William Cobbold was Master he brewed beer in the workhouse for those who

---

[43] East Kent Gazette July 18th 1865

were ill instead of buying it in and this was cheaper. Sometimes the doctor prescribed wine for the sick too as it was thought to strengthen the constitution.

By the early 1900s rhubarb grown on the workhouse land was stewed and served to the children and the sick, and lettuce was grown and given at supper time to the inmates, indeed most of the vegetables consumed in the workhouse were grown there. It was in 1901 that a new rota of dinners was agreed for the workhouse and this was to be:

Sunday	cold roast beef and vegetables instead of bread and cheese
Monday	beef broth and bread instead of boiled beef and vegetables
Tuesday	boiled mutton and vegetables instead of pea soup and bread
Wednesday	barley soup and bread instead of bread and cheese
Thursday	bacon or pork and vegetables instead of suet pudding and vegetables
Friday	meat and vegetables instead of pea soup and bread.[44]

Illness and Healthcare

From the start a doctor was paid to attend the workhouse inmates but there were no nurses; instead unpaid untrained inmates did the job. This was soon to change as

---

[44] East Kent Gazette Jan 5 1901

the need for paid nurses became evident although it would be many years before the nurses were trained.

In 1839 the Board of Guardians were concerned that the general state of the workhouse was unsatisfactory owing to a lack of discipline and proper organising of cleaning by the Master, Oliver Alderton and his wife Elizabeth, the Matron. So they were given three months to satisfy the Board that they were able to improve matters or be given their notice. The lack of cleanliness led to 'an eruption amongst the inmates' of skin infections and the Medical Officer, local surgeon Mr George Ray was called in and given the freedom to treat the dozen worst cases as he wished. After two months it was noted that both the clothes and the dormitories were cleaner.

We cannot know the details of how the sick were cared for, but it is clear that all was not well under the Aldertons. Yet, when allegations of neglect leading to death were made, the Guardians dismissed them out of hand. A poor couple, the Cawsons, had reported that one of the inmates, George Stiles had died because of neglect but 'the Master, Mistress and Nurses proved to the satisfaction of the Guardians that every attention had been paid to Stiles'.

In addition to appointing a medical officer to attend the inmates of the workhouse, every union area had medical officers who attended the poor who were sick in their own homes. In the case of the Milton Union three doctors were at first appointed, one having the workhouse as part of his responsibilities. For some years medical officers could not prescribe medicines but simply dietary supplements such as meat or porter.

In 1840 new regulations for vaccination came into force. Vaccination of the population against smallpox was the responsibility of the Guardians. The union was divided into three districts and allocated to three doctors. Dr Imlach and Mr Grayling, surgeon, both of Sittingbourne, were to have the Milton and Sittingbourne districts. They would carry out vaccinations once a week at their homes and once a month at the vestry room in Bredgar church.

Those paupers who were mentally ill could be kept in workhouses or if they were severe cases sent to asylums. The Milton Union sent most of its serious cases to the Kent Lunatic Asylum at Barming and a few to Bethlem (Bedlam) Hospital in London where they were paid for by the Union. Isaac Skilder was one of those who went to Bethlem and was maintained there for some years in the 1840s. It was more expensive to send the mentally ill to asylums so if they were manageable they were kept in the workhouse.

From 1842 the law required regular inspections by so-called Commissioners in Lunacy of the mentally ill or mentally handicapped people who were kept in the workhouse. The 1879 inspection found two inmates of each sex of unsound mind,[45] one of them was a young girl called Mary Ann Wheeler. She was 'the subject of Melancholia' and the Master was advised to watch her carefully as she might be suicidal. She was to be sent to an asylum. All the patients were found to be dressed satisfactorily and were 'evidently under kind treatment'. The inspector considered the workhouse clean and well ventilated and only criticised the fact that the patients continued to have straw mattresses and pillows and had less meat in their diet than he thought appropriate.

---

[45] CKS G/Mi ACa

Many families struggled to support their mentally ill or handicapped relatives at home. Such a one was Stephen Baker of Milton who in desperation wrote to the Poor Law Board in London for help:

> *'I Stephen Baker beg to apply to you respecting the state of my son George Albert Baker who is now and always has been quite an Idiot, he is very much subjected to strong fits and often falls down in the roads or any other places....to risk of his life. I have made several applications to the Guardians round here for some relief but had no assistance....he is now 23....I am 58.... my wife is laid up with Rheumatism. I have been in the habit of earning 3-4 shillings a day.. my character is well known...I never spend a penny in luxury or in waste....'*

The local Wesleyan minister added a sentence to say that Mr Baker was a well respected member of his congregation.[46]

For the long-term sick in the workhouse the days must have passed with a dreadful slow tedium with nothing but each other's company to divert them in their crowded bare dormitories. If bed-bound they would have had to lie in the same position for hours without sufficient pillows to be propped up. There were no soft chairs to sit in for awhile to relieve their aches and pains.

The small number of toilets and lack of drainage made the workhouse a smelly and unhealthy place and the Master was reminded in 1842 to use chloride of lime 'to prevent them being offensive'. Infections often broke out and spread rapidly amongst the inmates, so in 1849 in the midst of a cholera epidemic, the Finance Committee met

---

[46] ibid

with the medical officer at the workhouse to plan how a more suitable infirmary could be provided. They agreed that nothing could be done usefully within the existing building even by adding a storey and noted that at Milton they had 'so far escaped the dangerous consequences of infectious diseases in a crowded workhouse where the inmates may be expected to be peculiarly susceptible to such influences, the result of their own previous bad habits'.[47] No acknowledgement in that of the shortcomings of the sanitation but only of the dirty habits of the inmates.

The committee recommended buying the old Milton parish workhouse as it was separate but very close by. The owner was ready to sell. Cholera broke out in the area generally that summer and the medical officer, Mr Ray wrote to the Guardians; 'As the Asiatic Cholera has broken out in the house I beg to recommend that for the present all the inmates be allowed fresh meat daily'.[48] In this way he obviously hoped to build up their strength and resistance to disease. This was adopted with eight ounces of meat given to the adults and four to the children. A few days later an extraordinary meeting was called by two of the Guardians to discuss whether the inmates should be removed from the workhouse. They heard the following report from Mr Ray:

> 'Gentlemen
>
> *After an anxious week I hope I may congratulate you on the gradual subsidence of the epidemic in the Milton Union. Only one new case has occurred during the last 24 hours. Almost all the inmates, Adults as well as*

---

[47] CKS G/MiAM4

[48] ibid

children, have been suffering more or less from Diarrhoea but at this time there are but six cases of cholera in the house and with two exceptions these cases are progressing favourably.

From the commencement there have been in the house 30 cases of malignant cholera, of these eight have died but of that number six were aged and of worn out constitutions. We have lost but two children and they were known beforehand to be of feeble constitution. This is a small number when it is taken into account that without exception all the young and most of the old have suffered from the premonitory symptoms. I attribute this small mortality to the prompt measures used. The remedies were always at hand and the House Staff from the Master down to the humblest of the nurses have one and all manifested the greatest promptitude and kindness in carrying out my wishes.

There is now the question what shall be done with those who remain in the House. I would beg to suggest all attempts to remove them en masse must be abandoned. The thing is impracticable and if it were practicable it would not be desirable for they would carry with them the greatest terror. Let all available means be used to disperse people by allowing out-door relief on a <u>liberal scale</u>. They will not carry infection with them, change of air will cheer their spirits as well as renovate their bodies and in a few weeks they may be re-assembled without danger.'

A copy was sent to the Poor Law Board.

The Guardians took Mr Ray's advice and all inmates who wished to leave could do so provided they could obtain accommodation satisfactory to the Master and were given 4/- a week each. Then volunteers were sought to stay in the workhouse as nurses. Seven male inmates came forward: George Milway, James Fawkener, William Greenstreet, Tim Wills, John Roberts, Stephen Mills and John Eason and they were paid two shillings a day for their work. Three women volunteered as nurses; Ann Curtis, Fanny Johnson and Francis Ellis and they were paid the same amount.

The following week the building committee was ordered to examine the drains and privies to make sure all was in order and Mr Ray reported that all the staff were much fatigued and had been confined to the building. So it was ordered that they be allowed to leave in detachments for change and rest. The Poor Law Board requested weekly reports on the epidemic and the clerk wrote to them to ask if there would be any help for the union with the extra expenses which the outbreak had entailed. By August the drains were being improved and the 'Dead House' (as the mortuary was known) was demolished and a new one provided. The inmates returned and the dietary declined from the dizzy heights of meat every day to meat every other day.

The Guardians decided that they should show their appreciation of the great efforts made by the staff during the epidemic and so they voted gratuities 'for active exertions and unremitting attention shown to the inmates during the cholera.' For Mr Ray there was £10, for his assistant £5, for the Master and Matron, William and Lucy Cobbold, £6 each, for the two teachers £5 each and the same for the porter and the matron's assistant. Then there was the chaplain who had attended the sick and dying most faithfully. For him it was felt that a letter rather than money might be appropriate and so the clerk wrote 'to express to the Rev. William Brewer 'the high sense they entertain of the very kind care and attention shown by him to the inmates during the cholera - a period during which the extraordinary duties devolving on him which he so conscientiously discharged exposed him to trials of a most painful nature as well as circumstances of no ordinary peril'.

In the autumn there was a further outbreak of cholera at Rainham and the Guardians hired a house there for use as a cholera hospital.[49]

When Mr Ray died all the Guardians attended his funeral and recorded their appreciation of the twenty years of 'zeal, humanity and benevolence' with which he had carried out his tasks for the poor.[50] His son was appointed in his place. One or two of the other area medical officers proved less satisfactory than Mr Ray; Mr Friend was asked for his resignation after a disagreement with the Guardians. He had apparently ordered mutton for sick paupers without getting their authorisation. They also wanted to know if he had ordered gin without telling them.[51]

---

[49] CKS G/MiAM4
[50] CKS G/MiAM6
[51] CKS G/MiAM5

This part of the 1840 tithe map of Milton shows the workhouse on the edge of the town surrounded by open land.(Reproduced with the permission of the Centre for Kentish Studies)

Dr Penfold annoyed the Guardians many times in the 1860s by not sending in the required weekly medical reports and not responding to their questions. He was not only slip-shod with the paper work though but there were also doubts about whether he performed his duties properly. One hapless woman, Elizabeth White of Rainham, gave birth in the cart on the way to the workhouse. In view of this the Guardians wondered whether he could really have visited her as he said.

The workhouse would remain a remarkably perilous place to live in until the basic sanitation of the building was improved. There was a further outbreak of cholera in the district in 1854 which rapidly infected the workhouse and this was an occasion when the conscientious and serious manner in which Sir John Tylden carried out his duties as chairman of the Guardians was most apparent. He or the vice chairman, George Eley, visited the Union daily for the two months of the outbreak to support the Master and make decisions with the medical officer.

Sanitary conditions in the House remained very poor with just small improvements such as the installation in the infirmary in 1863 of a 'White and Company Patent Self-Acting Earth Closet'. Reporting in 1867 an inspector found[52] that the sick wards were very small with 'an objectionable arrangement for the water closets in each, which are merely partitioned off in the corner by a wooden partition.' He found all the drainage very deficient, there were no proper lavatories at all, and the boys still washed in a sink in the yard. The nurse was the cook, so there was still a lack of trained medical care.

In 1869 there was again much illness amongst the inmates and one of the Guardians took a sample of the water to have it analysed, fearing that it was polluted by sewage. A pump to provide a constant stream of water was then installed which would have helped but not solved the

---

[52] NA MH12 5281

problem. The threat of infectious illness remained a recurring feature of workhouse life so in an attempt to reduce the spread of such diseases an infectious ward was added in 1874 where patients with small pox or typhoid could be nursed away from others. But perversely its drains ran straight into the brook in the grounds. The drains from the boys school room also ran straight into the stream in the grounds until a year later. That was the year when the decision was made that all the privies be converted to earth closets and galvanised iron receptacles were installed.

In March 1881 the Local Government Board which had taken over responsibility for workhouses received a report from their inspector on his visit to the Milton workhouse. He reported 14 cases of typhoid fever since Christmas of which six inmates died. The Master and Matron had themselves fallen ill with the disease.[53] The outbreak had begun with the admission of a family from Lower Halstow who were already infected. It was then picked up by 'some of the inmates who were in an emaciated condition'. This shocking phrase comes from the report of the medical officer and implies that as late as the 1880s some people had half starved before they entered the workhouse. Indeed a few people still died of starvation in the countryside as a man did in Leeds near Hollingbourne in 1885.[54]

The Board requested a report from the Guardians on the situation and recommended that they should press on with the erection of the infectious hospital as rapidly as possible and then convert the workhouse infectious ward to sick wards. The Guardians were keen to build as

---

[53] East Kent Gazette Apr 2 1881
[54] CKS G/Hb AM9

requested.[55] In addition they felt that it was absolutely vital that the workhouse should be provided for in the drainage scheme which was about to be constructed by the Urban Sanitary Authority, and this could be done if they contributed towards the scheme.

A month later in April 1881 we learn from one of the detailed reports of the weekly Guardians meetings published in the local paper, that pigs were kept at the workhouse, very close to the infectious wards. The Guardians were divided over the idea that they might be a health risk and should be moved further away but after a vote they agreed to the move. At last in 1883 the infectious hospital was built at Keycol Hill and the infectious wards of the workhouse were back in use as general wards.

Even by the late 1880s the sanitation of the workhouse was not yet all it could have been as the minutes of 1889 show.[56] One of the water-millers of Milton, Mr Bates, complained of an obstruction to the tail water of his mill, a stone alleged to have been placed in the stream on the workhouse premises. When the Guardians looked into the matter they found that the stream had been dammed at that point for many years, but when the new drainage scheme for the workhouse was carried out in 1883 it had been arranged that the water could be directed from the stream at the south-west corner of the main building and turned into the large sewer through the premises to help flush the system. It was agreed to lower the stone to answer the miller's concerns.

---

[55] CKS G / Mi / Mi ACa
[56] CKS G / Mi AM 17

Inevitably many inmates died in the workhouse and Lawrence Seager the Milton undertaker frequently brought his horse and hearse to the gate with the empty coffin and pall. He provided bearers for the funerals and charged the union a little over £2 for each adult funeral and half that for a child.

Guardians and Officers

There were twenty Guardians for the eighteen parishes in the union because Sittingbourne and Milton with their far larger populations, were each entitled to two. Magistrates who lived in the area could sit on the board as ex-officio Guardians. The Tylden family of Milstead in the shape of Sir John Maxwell Tylden held sway over the board for many years and he was unswerving in his attendance as chairman. In later years his nephew Richard Tylden was chairman. It was not uncommon for one family to have such influence on a board, for the system was such that the same people tended to be elected year in year out. In many cases this could lead to matters always being dealt with in the same economical way, without any idea of change or reform.

The Guardians were elected by the rate payers and as time went on they put advertisements in the local paper to explain why they should be voted for. So for example in 1901[57] Charles Burley gave these reasons to the men of Sittingbourne:

*'Working Men should vote for Burley
Because he supported the new Dietary List,
Better food and more of it.*

---

[57] East Kent Gazette Mar 23 1901

> *Because he supported the Master having powers to allow out during the day those inmates who are well behaved and trustworthy*
> *Because he had always supported adequate out-relief being granted to the deserving poor*
> *Because he is not afraid to express his views and act up to them'.*

From 1844 the Guardians had elected a finance committee of five from amongst themselves.

The Guardians employed a full time clerk who worked at the workhouse. There was weekly correspondence to be dealt with from the Poor Law Commissioners, from the parishes, and from other unions as well as the minutes of the Guardians' meetings to write.

After some years Boards of Guardians also acted as the Rural Sanitary Authority. Their work in this guise did not directly concern the workhouse but was to do with roads, drainage, sewers and so on. Their influence therefore spread into the wider community so it is little wonder that their election became even more a matter for local politics.

Out-Relief and Relieving Officers

The relieving officers of the union had very responsible positions for which they were each paid the considerable salary of £100 a year. They were required to visit each parish weekly, placing a list of those receiving out-relief that week on the church door, and giving out the bread or flour and money. They had to decide which applicants for relief were genuine and which were not and report their decisions to the Guardians. Two were appointed when the Milton Union was set up in 1835, John Vinton whose area covered Bobbing, Borden. Lower Halstow, Hartlip Iwade, Newington, Rainham and Upchurch and Thomas Tarpe who had the rest of the parishes.

To begin with, as the Guardians and relieving officers got used to the new Act, there were cases where they were uncertain of procedure. One such was whether a woman of 66 could be given out-relief because she owned a mangle. The implication of this was that she should have been able to keep herself by taking in washing. In 1845 a complaint was made by several Guardians that the relieving officer did not visit all the parishes weekly and that the poor had to walk many miles to collect their due. They resolved that the officers must weekly relieve the poor of Borden in that parish as soon as they found a covered place for the purpose. And that the officer was to be present when the relief was given and see the bread and flour weighed to prevent any dispute.

The payment of out-relief could never entirely stop as the under-paid poor were too numerous to be housed in workhouses. Total expenditure on out-relief for the union area was steady at about £45 a week in 1839, dropping to £41 p.w. through 1840 and 1841. In December that year it went up to £45 p.w., up to £53 a week briefly in February 1843 and it climbed to £65 a week in October 1844. The dips and rises followed the fortunes of farming and the weather.

Able-bodied men were the only class of paupers for whom out-relief was strictly prohibited. They had to enter the workhouse if they required help, but in some areas of Kent this could not be adhered to because of the scale of hardship encountered. Some Kentish Unions such as

Hollingbourne had so many farm labourers out of work that they did not have room to admit them in the bad winters of 1838 and 1841. They were obliged to give 240 families money and bread in their homes. The Poor Law Commissioners allowed other exceptions to their rule of no out-relief for the able-bodied and these were temporary sickness, burials, and the first months of widowhood. They wished out-relief to be paid at least partially in goods. In fact time proved that out-relief for the able-bodied could not be completely abolished.

The clerk noted regularly in the minute book when temporary out-relief was given to able-bodied men who were unable to work for a while through illness, as when Richard Saywell a carpenter of Milstead had a fever in 1841, or in the same year when William Fullager a labourer of Borden had inflammation of the lungs.

Occasional large expenses such as funerals caused difficulty to families who otherwise managed independently. And so it was in Milton when Stephen Chrisfield's child died and he applied for a loan of three shillings to assist in the burial. It was granted.

By 1850 the out-relief was set for adults at one shilling and eight pence and one gallon of flour a week and children were to have either the money or the flour.

We know very little of the large number of poor who were given regular small payments in out-relief. However, if the recipients had no official settlement in the Milton union area then letters had to be written by the clerk to have their out-relief payments authorised by their home union who would then have to refund the money. So it was that when in 1845 old Thomas Vicks whose settlement was Hereford, was unable to support himself in Milton without assistance, the clerk wrote to that union asking for authorisation. More usually the recipients belonged to other Kentish unions and had not journeyed so far from their place of origin as Vicks. Sometimes questions arose as to whether a recipient of out-relief was actually entitled by settlement to receive it. The Guardians had doubts in the case of Angelina Syfleet who claimed to be of Borden and she was brought before them to answer questions in 1848.

In 1865 a Poor Law Inspector came to Milton to enquire into two charges of neglect against the relieving officer Walter Strouts. The charges were brought by the Rev. English then vicar of Milton, who was a member of the board and a thorn in the flesh of the other Guardians. The enquiry was reported in the local paper, courtesy of English himself who had pressed for a journalist to be allowed into meetings. When this was refused he promised to deliver strictly impartial reports himself. However these reports lasted only a few months as so many complaints were received by the paper about English's bias. Presumably he was too humane for the penny pinching Guardians.

Nevertheless the reports give us details of the out-relief then being given. One case concerned was that of Elizabeth Bean of Milton. She was in her eighties and was receiving one shilling and eight pence weekly plus a gallon of flour to make bread. She was frail, and a young girl who lived in the same house came to collect it for her. Walter Strouts gave out the money and the tickets for flour every Thursday afternoon in Milton and the poor then took their tickets to get the flour from the miller. One of the complaints against Strouts was that he had been leaving the out-relief for the four Tunstall recipients at Bredgar instead of taking it all the way to Tunstall. Strouts defended himself and the inspector found something to criticise on both sides, nevertheless Strouts did not keep the job much longer.

1870 found the Guardians criticised by the Poor Law Board for giving too much out-relief to able-bodied men. The inspector called again and this time he recommended using the chapel and the rooms above it as receiving wards to make more room for the able-bodied. So 24 more beds were purchased and more oakum for picking and the men were refused out-relief.

The Guardians judged the morals of those who applied and if applicants were found wanting they were refused relief as was the case with a widow with several children whose relief was discontinued in 1881 as she had recently given birth to an illegitimate child.

In March 1890 a great number of men were thrown out of work in Milton due to a strike of bargemen and a lock-out of brick makers. There were far too many to admit to the workhouse and so to justify paying them out-relief, the Guardians issued an order prescribing a task of work to be done under the care of a superintendent. It was that they should all either break stones from 7am to 5 pm, or grub stones, or dig, with a one hour break for dinner.[58]

Vagrants

From the start a constant stream of wandering poor, in search of a bed, turned up at the doors of the workhouse where they were entitled to stay for one night. Numbers of vagrants in Kent always swelled in the autumn for the harvest and many of these wandering people were Irish.

---

[58] CKS G / MiAM17

Workhouses such as Milton which had been built very soon after the 1834 Act, possessed no purpose-built wards for vagrants or casuals as they were known. Before further wards were added sheds were used. A purpose-built male vagrants ward was in place at Milton by 1842, but the glass windows were repeatedly broken by the troublesome men and so were soon covered with wire. Vagrants were treated as the lowest of the low and had to work for their night's accommodation before they were free to leave next morning.

With the new Master in post in 1843 this was the time to tighten up on procedures and make sure the vagrants all carried out their tasks, so a police constable was to be sent for to make sure they did so and if not then they were taken before a J.P. Records show that they were then often punished with twenty-one days hard labour. The men were to break a yard of stone which when broken each piece should be no bigger than two inches; or to wheel two yards of stone to the depot. If they were not up to this then, like the women, they would have to pick a pound of oakum or a pound and a half of coconut fibre for mats.

In the early years the porter was disturbed late at night by tramps knocking to be let in with the ticket of admittance that the relieving officer had given them, but in 1843 the Guardians agreed that except in cases of great emergency no one would be admitted after 9pm.

The conditions in the vagrants' wards were the most basic it is possible to imagine. An inspector in 1867 found that the men's ward was only a stable, and the beds merely benches with straw on them and a rag for cover.[59] They were treated like animals.

---

[59] NA MH12 5281

From 1860 a general rise in the number of vagrants in the county began and continued for the next thirty years. New receiving wards were built at Milton in 1869 and a few years later permission was given for casual wards for females to be built. The number of inmates in the workhouse peaked in December 1879 at 188. The resultant overcrowding was exacerbated by the fact that a fire which started in the laundry drying room had damaged two dormitories. The winter of 1880 found the Guardians looking for extra accommodation in the house. They came up with a temporary solution which was renting a new Sittingbourne oast house for a month and putting beds in it. The vagrants comprised not only men but women and children too. In one week in May 1880 of the 163 vagrants 36 were women and 25 children.

The severe attitude of the local public and press towards the vagrants is exemplified by an editorial in the East Kent Gazette that winter which stated that, 'it would be a good rule if a man would not work neither should he eat at the expense of the general community' and went on to blame the fact that they would not work because of the subsistence they could get from going from one workhouse to another. 'Perhaps in the case of Milton Union the comfortable quarters provided for them induces these people to favour Milton with their presence.' The writer did concede that if no food were given many would starve but felt that the tramps should be kept long enough to work sufficiently to pay for what they had been given, by stone breaking and oakum picking. Which is of course what happened. The editorial concluded by recommending the return of the stocks for men who would not work.

During just one week in September 1881, 275 vagrants were relieved.[60] This was by no means exceptional at harvest time; there were on average a hundred less a week in the spring. The total number of vagrants who were admitted into the Milton wards in that year was 6968, which was a considerable increase on the previous year. The Guardians found it necessary to extend the receiving wards again in 1896. By 1904 numbers had declined to the still considerable total of over a thousand a year.

It was rare indeed for anyone outside the workhouse to interest themselves in the vagrants, but in 1890 a Miss Barnett sent a parcel of texts and books for use in the casual wards.

Financing the Workhouse

Until 1865 payments were made by each parish in the union, calculated by the number of paupers from each parish, the number of days they were in the workhouse and the clothing and provisions issued. So for example in one quarter of 1841 Bredgar had 30 inmates staying a total of 1,971 days requiring £36 of provisions and £8 of clothes. Poor rate defaulters were regularly summonsed in all the parishes. A close eye was kept on the expenditure at the workhouse. The Master kept accounts of all he spent and the books were examined weekly by the clerk. Local tradesmen tendered to supply the institution with goods such as flour, coal or candles and the Guardians decided which to accept.

---

[60] East Kent Gazette Sep 3 1881

As well as ensuring the best commercial deals, the Guardians also ensured that local men face their responsibilities if they had fathered children. So in 1840 the Guardians applied to the Petty Sessions held at the Lion Inn, Sittingbourne, for an order on Edmund Randall of Wormshill, a labourer, to make him pay maintenance for his baby born to Mary Lambkin of Bredgar in the workhouse. This was just one of many such cases dealt with in this way so that the charge of the child did not fall on the ratepayers.

But still sometimes men went off leaving their wives and children in the workhouse at the charge of the ratepayers as happened in the case of Henry Milway, a Milton man in 1839, and then a warrant was obtained from the magistrates for his arrest. Proceedings were taken on the same occasion against George King of Throwley for not obeying the magistrates order for the maintenance of his father who was chargeable to Tunstall parish. George Satteen left his family in the workhouse chargeable to Tong. George and his family went in and out over the next few years, George being uncooperative and refusing to work when he was inside.

In 1865 the Union Chargeability Act transferred the total cost of poor relief from the parish to the union to better balance the inequality between rich and poor parishes within unions. In 1870 a Poor Law Board inspector came to discuss the state of pauperism in the Milton union; to check how many people were being assisted outside the workhouse or kept in it and what the costs were. The clerk wrote up the information in the Guardians' minute book. They showed that the population had risen considerably in line with national trends. The figures which they had to use were well out of date coming as they did from the 1861 census which gave a figure of

14,775 as the total resident population of the parishes in the union area. Poor rate expenditure of every kind for the year 1868 was £12,204 and the average weekly amount of out-relief given to each pauper was one shilling and nine pence. The inspector considered these figures satisfactory, in spite of the rise in real expenditure, because that was inevitable with a larger population.

Spiritual Matters

Each workhouse had a chaplain so that services could be held in the workhouse to be attended by all inmates on Sundays. Few workhouses were built with a chapel though many were added later. Often the dining hall was used for services as was the case at Milton. A purpose built chapel was added in a corner of the grounds in 1876. It was very plain; the first stained glass window showing 'the Good Shepherd', was not put in for another 25 years.

An effort was made to improve the spiritual state of the paupers when 500 copies of 'The Poor Man's Friend' were given out by the Guardians in 1841 and from 1844 there were Bibles available to read which were given by the British and Foreign Bible Society.

In 1892 the Rev. Abdiel Hanham resigned as chaplain after 25 years. When the ministers of the Baptist, Congregational and Methodist churches of Sittingbourne and Milton knew he was to leave, they offered to conduct a service in the workhouse chapel every Thursday evening at no charge. The Guardians did not allow it. They felt that 'the existing regulations for preservation of liberty of conscience in matters of religion are amply sufficient'.[61] Perhaps they feared that the ministers would be interfering in matters which did not concern them.

The Rev. William Bond took up the chaplaincy. He performed a short service for the sick in the wards on Sunday mornings followed by a full service in the chapel. He gave communion once a month and visited the workhouse two days a week to see the sick and elderly. In cases of serious illness he came more frequently.

The Guardians' strictly limited idea of what was suitable spiritual fare for their charges continued and in 1901 and 1903 they refused to allow the Salvation Army to hold regular services in the infirmary. They did however relent so far as to allow Milton Congregational Free Church choir to sing there in 1904.

Sailors and Soldiers

Milton Creek, where barges docked daily, to load and unload their cargoes, lay close by to the Union house, so it comes as no surprise to find local sailors such as Israel Friday, John Irons and Edward Durant amongst the early inmates of the Union.

Then too there were old soldiers, disabled in various ways, who had served their country during the Napoleonic wars and were not able to make ends meet on their pensions. John Cooper (also known as John Wood), was a pensioner from the 49th regiment of infantry who did not take kindly to workhouse life. He proved to be a rebellious inmate for he had to be threatened with an appearance before the magistrate because he refused to

---

[61] CKS G / MiAM 17

pick oakum in 1839.[62] On another occasion he was taken before the magistrates for running out of the House, returning in the night and getting in by climbing over the roof. He drank himself into a stupor a few years later and the clerk noted 'That John Cooper be taken before a magistrate when he is well enough for having squandered £3-12-2, the balance of his pension, in two days.'[63] The amount of alcohol which could have been purchased for that money then is staggering!

William Mitchell came into the union house with his wife and children in 1839 and stayed for many years so he must have been an invalid. He had a small pension from the Sheerness Dockyard which was paid towards his keep while he was an inmate.

In 1871 the Guardians received a letter via the Admiralty from William Hoby on HMS Fawn at Panama regarding the support of his wife who was then in the workhouse.[64] Hoby wrote with heart-felt indignation:

> *"I object to support her because she deceived me at the time of our marriage, she being then pregnant with a child born six months after marriage, she at the time confessing John Scofield of the Royal Engineers was the father. Debts have been contracted which have not been made known to me through her, but Bills sent to me by different trades people to £3 and my clothes and furniture parted with. It was my intention to obtain a Divorce, but could not do so on account of the short time the ship was at Sheerness."*

---

[62] CKS G/ MiAM2

[63] CKS G/MiAM3

[64] CKS G / Mi / ACa

The Admiralty stated that under the circumstances it was not in its power to make him pay. No doubt the Guardians then made enquiries about John Scofield.

The Elderly

Although there were always more elderly poor on out-relief than those who were inmates, yet the infirm elderly also formed a large percentage of the long-term inhabitants of workhouses. Most, in those days before old-age pensions, regarded the workhouse with fear and dread. Once admitted they would spend years inside with little to do to pass their days or break up the depressing tedium. In the early years the wards were spartan with bare walls, lime washed every couple of years, containing only beds, and a bench or perhaps hard backed chairs. After a few years a cupboard was put in the old women's ward so that they could keep their little bit of tea and sugar in there.

Across England after 1870 a little more accommodation was provided for elderly married couples to share a room in workhouses, though it was still uncommon, and before this date was very rare indeed for a couple to have a room together. A discussion by the Milton board, reported in the local paper in 1879,[65] makes it clear that the Guardians were aware that married couples could request a shared room but none did. It is likely that they were not informed that such provision could be made.

For those who could read there was very little available although in 1839 the chaplain persuaded the Guardians to spend £5 on books for the inmates. Many years later in

---

[65] East Kent Gazette Jul 12 1879

1870 the Guardians had a box placed in Sittingbourne station so that passengers could place the newspapers they had read in it, so that at least the inmates could have some stale news.

It was rare indeed for any special occasion to change the tedious daily round for the residents and so it must have been a very great pleasure for them to be invited by George Smeed to a rural fete in the grounds of his home at Gore Court Park on the edge of Sittingbourne in 1859. They were brought in wagons and on arrival each was given a glass of wine, tobacco for the men and in the evening a pint of ale and some fruit. This became an annual event, and a substantial tea was always given to the inmates in specially erected tents in the park. Then there was a band to listen to and races to watch. Smeed, who was a Guardian for many years, organised the fetes for the poor of the area and the inmates of the workhouse and they proved vastly popular. In 1879 there were estimated to be 8000 people at the fete, indicating how the appeal of the event had widened to include the general public. By then a committee was needed to organise it and attractions included a steam roundabout and substantial prizes for the races, which included a three mile bicycle event.

Christmas, 1879 brought an unusual extra treat for the inmates. There was singing and a production of a comic play entitled 'A rough diamond,' by the staff including the Master and Matron, Mr and Mrs Black.[66] Herbert and Sarah Black took charge of the Milton workhouse early in their lives, for when they arrived in 1877 they were only in their late twenties and full of energy.

---

[66] Eat Kent Gazette Jan 4 1879

In 1892 Milton Congregational Choir came to sing. That year the Guardians resolved that all the elderly men as well as the sick should be given half an ounce of tobacco a week and the elderly women an ounce of snuff.

By the 1890s the conditions for elderly inmates had improved, but workhouses were advised in 1896 to divide the aged according to their moral character and previous habits, granting those of good habit extra comforts and privileges, such as receiving visitors or going out during the day.

The advent of old age pensions in 1908 meant a great fall in the numbers of elderly on out-relief all over the country, but it did not cause a large drop in the numbers of elderly inmates since those inside were largely incapable of caring for themselves.

Emigration

There is no evidence in the records of the Milton Union of the large scale, assisted emigration which occurred during the 1840s in some Kentish unions such as Hollingbourne. References to emigrants at Milton are few and refer to individuals rather than groups of forty or fifty people as in the Hollingbourne Union. One of the first families to be assisted were the Crouchers; Thomas, his wife and six children from Bobbing were helped in 1838 to go to Canada.

In 1839 the clerk of the Board wrote to the Commissioners to enquire whether they would support two young brothers, James and Stephen Wakelin of Rainham emigrating to America as they were keen to go and came from a large family. This was refused.

In 1840 the Crayden family of Milton asked to be helped to emigrate to New Zealand. The advice of the Commissioners was later sought as to whether New Zealand was recognised as a British Colony and if so could paupers be sent there; the Commissioners replied that it was. The Guardians did help Sarah Ann Burnett and her two children to join her husband in New Zealand by providing clothing and conveyance to Deptford. The cost was then charged to her parish of Borden. In 1842 James Moore and his wife of Tong were helped to leave for a new life in Australia. That year two Ingram families from Borden left for Canada, John and Richard were brothers in their thirties and they and their wives and young families were assisted.

Ten years later two brothers from Tong, William and Joseph Hope, their wives and children were helped to emigrate to Canada.

Libel Against the Master

A local scandal erupted in 1874 when the then Master, Richard Kent, took out an action for damages against the Rev. William Harker, vicar of Milton. Richard Kent's case was that the vicar had published slanderous articles about him in the local paper, twice made allegations about him at public meetings, and had 200 placards printed which were libellous. So, totally denying all charges of misconduct, he was obliged to bring the case publicly to clear his name.[67] The Master, who had been in post less than two years, was known by all as a

---

[67] East Kent Gazette 25 July 1874

disciplinarian but the Guardians were satisfied with the good order that he brought to the workhouse.

The Rev. Harker's accusations were grave; he accused the Master of assaulting inmates, leaving a dead body indecently exposed and unattended, stealing vegetables grown at the workhouse and sending pork from the institution's pigs to his relatives in Sheffield. Harker's public speeches were delivered at the Assembly Rooms in Milton. One of the vicar's letters to the local paper had stated: 'great cruelty is exercised towards the poor inmates. For every trivial offence they are put upon a diet of bread and water for several days together. Assaults are common, persons are knocked down and kicked...' The Rev. Harker also found it suspicious that the Master had gone to Davington to be married rather than at Milton.

It was easy enough in court at Maidstone to show the accounts of surplus vegetables and pigs having been sold as usual and the money paid into workhouse funds. The body which had been left unclothed was proved to have been covered in the normal way. A number of ex-inmates appeared in court to say that they had been ill treated in the workhouse and had poor food. Their words reported verbatim[68] have the ring of truth, but their complaints were not of being assaulted but rather of harshness by the Master and the poor quality of the food.

Other matters came up in court including the case of an old man named Bowrey who was admitted to the workhouse with a note from the district medical officer, Dr Penfold, saying he was to go into the infirmary. But upon being examined by the workhouse medical officer Mr Ray, he was declared fit and told to pick oakum. This

---

[68] East Kent Gazette 1 Aug 1874

he refused to do and was threatened by the Master with being taken before the magistrate. So he left and took his complaint to Dr Penfold.

The judge was severe about Rev. Harker in his summing up remarking that 'a man in his position ought to be careful not to bear false witness against his neighbour.' He added that all the allegations should have been brought before the Board of Guardians not written in the press, a statement that it is hard to disagree with. The jury did not need to retire to deliver a verdict against the Rev. Harker on all counts and to award the Master £500 damages. It seems the vicar was either naïve in his ready belief in all that the poor people told him of their treatment, or else he was motivated by animosity against Richard Kent. In either case he did not use the correct channels to take his complaints forward. However we can also conclude that Richard Kent was a harsh Master whose regime led many inmates to hold a grudge against him and that the Milton inmates were lucky that he only worked there for five years.

A Model Workhouse?

It was many years before the conditions inside the workhouse could be considered in any way comfortable and if we had been able visit the wards in 1870 we would have found many aspects unchanged since the building opened. An inspector visited that year and was critical of much that he saw.[69] The women's toilets were exposed and all joined together, those for the boys were inadequate. Clothing and bedding were insufficient.

---

[69] CKS G/MiAM11

Some beds were too short. There were no mats between beds. The pillows of the sick inmates were stuffed with straw just the same as those of the able-bodied, nor did they have under blankets between the straw mattress and the under sheet.

Some inmates were having to eat their meals in their day wards. The sick wards and lying-in wards still only had cold taps. There were no hand rails on the stairs to the sick wards. Water-proof sheets were needed. There were no warm capes or gowns for the bed-ridden to wear. There were no mirrors anywhere. Industrial training for boys was insufficient. There was not enough accommodation for vagrants. There was no small bath for babies.

Upon reading this damning critique the Guardians selected a few of their number to consider it and report back on any action they considered necessary. They decided that divisions between each seat in the women's toilets should be put in as well as a door and window. The boys toilets should be provided with a basin. Extra clothing and bedding was ordered and just six warm capes and six dressing gowns, also the sick were to be given flock pillows and a small mirror placed in each ward. Short beds were to be lengthened (quite how one wonders!), and coconut matting placed between the beds. They agreed to have a hand-rail put on the stairs to the sick wards.

To create more space for eating meals the Guardians decided that for now the chapel could be used if ledges were placed along the back of the forms for tables. When it came to those recommendations which required a considerable expenditure the Guardians saw no way to avoid enlarging the vagrants wards, but they baulked at hot taps and saw nothing wrong with the training for the boys. It was to be another seventeen years before the Guardians were obliged by the Poor Law Board to make considerable improvements to the building.

During 1887 a great deal of hammering and banging disturbed the sick and elderly inmates of the workhouse for a large new addition to the building was being constructed at the heart of the workhouse. It was in the courtyard where the old receiving wards for casuals had stood. No trace of the new addition could be seen from the street where the façade of the building remained as bleak and dingy as ever. Yet the new building was 120 feet long and two storeys high, joined to the entrance hall by a corridor lit by gas lamps. A new kitchen with larder and store room, a new laundry and a boiler room for heating the building were located off the corridor. Everything was equipped in the most modern fashion, the kitchen containing four large steam boilers in which much of the food was cooked. There were also four large potato steamers and large ovens.

The laundry had space for seven women to work and all their hot water was heated by steam, it was equipped with a drying room too where the flat irons were kept. Further down the corridor was the dining hall large enough for 200 at a sitting. Old procedures were maintained in the new building for a wooden screen separated the men from the women and children as they ate and was 'an effectual preventative to any communication between the elderly folk;'[70] and there were separate entrances for the men and women. The building contained three flushing toilets and there were new sleeping wards for men upstairs.

---

[70] East Kent Gazette 29th Jan 1888

Outside, the open drains were at last all covered in. A new receiving ward for tramps was built adjoining the infirmary, and a new padded room for the mentally ill adjoined it. As a result of all the new building other parts of the workhouse were re-organised so that the old kitchen became a clothing store, the boys had a new bathroom in what was the old scullery and the old dining hall became a second day room for the men. The old women's day room was turned into an extra bedroom for the girls. What had been the laundry was the new nursery and the old nursery now served as the day room for the elderly women.

Of course such a total change in the workhouse had not originated with the Guardians but with the Local Government Board Inspector for the area, and once the scheme was agreed an architect was employed and then local builder Henry Tidy of Bell Road Sittingbourne was given the contract. The local paper was effusive in its praise for the results of the scheme: 'In such a well-appointed establishment, and with such a thoroughly efficient staff of officials, we repeat that the ratepayers of the Milton Union have indeed good reason for congratulation, and under its present regime there is every probability that it will continue to be what it certainly is - a model workhouse.'[71]

---

[71] East Kent Gazette 28th Jan 1888

PART THREE - 1900-1948
On the Edge of Change

The later years of the nineteenth century saw a gradual improvement in the standards of care and provision for the inmates at Milton, reflecting similar improvements nationally. For many years now it had been the case that workhouses were mainly filled with the aged and the sick, the orphaned and the mentally ill and not with the able-bodied out of work.

A letter from a Local Government Board Inspector to the Guardians in January 1901 throws light on the state of the workhouse at the turn of the century.[72] Following his inspection he raised his concern that the children should be removed from the workhouse to a more suitable environment. He had in mind the small family homes run by a house mother and father which had begun to be set up by various workhouses from the 1870s. He felt too that a class of the 'aged deserving poor' should be created who had special privileges, and that out-relief to the aged poor should be raised to an adequate level.

However the Guardians believed the children were well cared for within the workhouse, not only that, but for many years those inmates who were both old and deserving had had special privileges. The poor were still officially divided into 'undeserving' feckless people who had never worked hard and were not honest, and the deserving who had done their best to support themselves and led respectable lives. As to the question of out-relief the Guardians could reply that they had increased the payments as requested.

---

[72] CKS G / Mi AM 20

In 1902 a committee of Guardians was appointed to look at the heating of the workhouse[73] and before reporting back with their recommendations they visited the Ipswich workhouse which was considered to be the most up to date in England. At Milton the dining hall, receiving wards, children's wards and tramps' wards were all in the new building and well heated by steam pipes from the boiler. However the infirmary and rest of the workhouse was warmed by no less than fifty open fires. These fires caused many problems, for the coal store was small and its position meant that coal and ashes had to be brought through the main entrance and along the corridor.

The laundry was still done entirely by hand and now that there were so few able-bodied women within the workhouse, women from outside were employed to do it. The committee made several practical recommendations to improve the situation, one of the most important being that some old cottages at the south west of the building be pulled down and a steam laundry erected. New boilers were to be placed in the old laundry and the entire heating of the workhouse controlled from there.

The physical surroundings of the inmates were being improved but conditions were still bleak and the frustration of being a long-term inmate is well illustrated by the case of a blind young man who in 1901 was reported to have just one book with raised letters which he read again and again. The Guardians resolved to provide him with a Bible for the blind.

---

[73] CKS / G / MiAM20

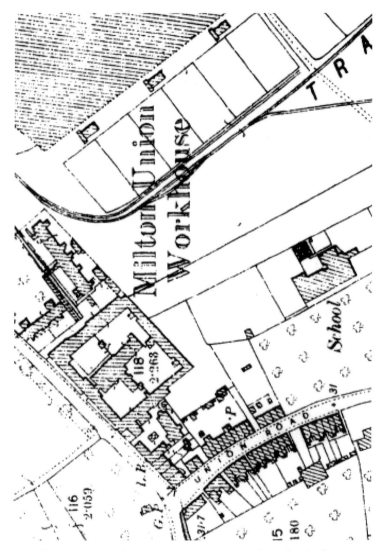

On this 1897 Ordnance Survey map the shaded area to the right of the workhouse is the brick works and the tram way for the bricks can be seen curving round the edge of the workhouse. The new building can be seen in the courtyard

Administration

In 1909 the Board of Guardians was meeting weekly at Sittingbourne Town Hall and this continued until 1912 when the new board room at the workhouse was complete.

Over the years the administration of the workhouse could be seen to have developed so that there were three committees: assessment, finance and school attendance.

There were three medical officers for the union area. Dr Edward Marmion attended the patients within the workhouse and the poor in Bobbing, Borden, Iwade and Milton whilst Dr Fisher and Dr Penfold divided the remaining parishes between them.

In 1915 there was for the first time a female Guardian elected to serve on the board, Mrs Alice Harvey. This was late compared to other unions since women had been eligible to serve since the 1870s but it was in the cities that most had been elected.

Clothes

Until 1913 all the cloth used to make the inmates clothes was striped, so there was striped cotton shirting, grey calico, linsey wolsey, and white flannel. Even the sheets were striped. But in 1913 the Guardians decided to follow the lead of others unions in discontinuing the stripe partly on the grounds that it would be cheaper. Gradually they introduced tweed jackets and waistcoats for the men with brown cord trousers. The boys were now to have a tweed suit for Sundays, tweed jackets and waistcoats and brown cord 'knickers'(short trousers), for weekdays. In 1914 Thomas Nelson was appointed tailor at the workhouse on £35 a year with lodgings, food and his washing done. It was then his job to make the clothes for the inmates, but only a year later in 1915 the Guardians were for the first time considering the provision of ready made clothing and shoes for the inmates on the grounds of cheapness.

The Children

A sign of the great improvement in the educational opportunities of the workhouse children, came when a boy called Arthur Wilson gained a scholarship to Borden School in 1901. The Guardians agreed he could be boarded out and supplied with suitable clothes for two years.[74] The children did however remain subject to rigorous discipline in the institution. When two twelve year olds, John Seager and Stephen Heathfield began to loiter about on their way back from school in 1902, the Master was instructed to give them a dozen strokes each with a birch rod. John Seager continued rebellious and absconded from the house a year later; on return he was birched again.

In 1905 Church House, a spacious old farm house next to Milton church, (now known as Green Porch), was leased by the workhouse as a home for girls and there they lived

---

[74] CKS G/MiAM20

under the care of a house mother.⁷⁵ The house had space for 37 girls.

Green Porch today (B. Allinson)

Church House came with a farm which the Guardians let out. The boys remained in the workhouse, but by 1912 plans were afoot for a separate home for them too. A committee was formed from amongst the Guardians to look into the purchase of Milton Brewery, Brewery House and cottages in Brewery Road. The Old Brewery was demolished before purchase and the site cleared for a new house which could take 25 boys; at this time there were 44 boys in the workhouse. Of these, 14 were under 7 and could go to the girls house whilst three were babies who would remain in the workhouse. The Guardians borrowed money and went ahead with the purchase in

---

⁷⁵ CKS G/MiAM21

1913. Foster parents were appointed and from the time the boys moved in, in 1914, the house was known as Langley House.[76]

The front of Bridge union workhouse in East Kent today. This was built to the same design of Sir Francis Head as the Milton Union. It is now attractively converted into flats and houses and the court yard is a garden (B. Allinson)

It had the advantage of standing beside the Butts school so the boys had no distance to go for school. Mr Lockyer who was brought up in Milton and attended the Butts remembers that many of the boys, in their distinctive grey workhouse uniforms, were amongst his friends. The local children did not consider themselves better than the workhouse children for many lived themselves in very poor circumstances. Mr Lockyer recalls that some of the workhouse boys went in every winter when their parent

---

[76] CKS G/MiAM23

could not find work and were taken out again in the summer.

Those children who were still in the care of the workhouse when they reached working age were found positions and given a new outfit. So Edith Anderson went into service in Park Road, Sittingbourne in 1922. Nearly every year a boy was apprenticed to be a fisherman at Ramsgate. George Bowes went in 1901 as did Albert Long in 1903.

In December 1900 a Mr Bowes wrote to invite the workhouse children to a matinee of 'Our Navy', a pantomime at the Town Hall, which was accepted. These invitations became annual events. The children began to receive more invitations from the surrounding townspeople. In 1902 they joined in the coronation festivities in Milton and a Fur and Feather show at the town hall in Sittingbourne and this too became an annual outing. Sittingbourne Football club invited the boys the same year to attend football matches in the town. In 1904 forty workhouse children were invited to a Milton Congregational Free Church Tea Party. Then there was an invitation to the Bobbing school treat the following year. Another sign of the times was that in 1906 some of the older boys were allowed to be taken to Sittingbourne swimming baths to be taught to swim. In the last years of the workhouse we hear of the children going on outings; in 1922 they were taken to Seasalter. That same year it was recommended that the boys be provided with nightshirts; they appear to have slept in their day shirts up to then.

Quite a number of Milton parents at this time were considered unfit to bring up their children due to their 'vicious habits', and the Guardians had the legal power, which they used, to take on all parental rights until the child became eighteen. So this was the equivalent of being taken into care today. Many examples could be quoted from this period for Milton, often involving several brothers and sisters. Sometimes the decision was made with orphans to maintain them in a national children's home as happened to the Crayden brothers, William and Thomas in 1914.[77] By 1915, 15 children had been adopted.

Work Inside the Workhouse

In 1900 the Master entered sales that he made in the ledger as usual. That year he had sold oakum, bones, vegetables and wood. There was an extra three-quarters of an acre of land at Church House where soft fruit was grown and an orchard, and this fresh produce was added to the inmates diet. Thousands of pounds of vegetables were grown on the workhouse land each year.

The women continued to undertake the domestic tasks inside the workhouse such as the washing, but now they were paid a little. The 'scrubbers' as those who cleaned the floors were called, were paid 7d an hour by 1920.

Able-bodied vagrants were still given the task of stone crushing; they were required to crush 5cwt of flint using stone pounders. Ten new ones were purchased in 1905 and again in 1910.

After the First World War unemployment was very high and many unions gave out-relief on an unprecedented scale. During such periods of mass unemployment when workhouses were full, stone-breaking or oakum-picking

---

[77] CKS G/Mi AM24

work was set in 'labour yards' for men to earn out-relief. Extra ideas were required however, so in 1921 as emergency measures the Guardians decided the garden could be dug and trenched by the men and the stream which still ran through the lower garden cleared and scoured. The winter garden work could be started early and all the painting and decorating needed in the building could be done by the unemployed.

For the future they suggested trying to get a contract to fill in the trenches in the field used for military training at Grove End Farm, Tunstall. Another idea was to approach the council with a view to taking on road repairs and stone picking from the land. Single men were to work 50 hours a week for 17 shillings and sixpence whilst the married men would receive an additional seven shillings for their wife and two shillings for each child.[78]

In 1922 in Milton, the Guardians accepted the offer of a quantity of chalk flints from Smeed Dean and Co. at Highsted on the southern outskirts of Sittingbourne. The flints were to be broken at the pit. Able-bodied men in receipt on unemployment benefit would be required to work from 7am to 5 pm five days a week and half of Saturday. A foreman would supervise them. However the clerk of the Rural District Council felt that broken pit flints would not be suitable for road repair and advised Kentish rag stone would be needed. Three trucks of this was bought and delivered to Sittingbourne railway station.

---

[78] CKS G/MiAM25

Milton High Street circa 1900

In December the Guardians wrote to the Prime Minister, the local M.P and all the other boards of Guardians in Kent saying:

> 'That in the opinion of this Board of Guardians one of the most urgent duties of His Majesty's Government is to provide work for the unemployed so that all persons not unemployed and genuinely desiring work shall not continue to remain subject to demoralising effects of the unemployment dole. Also in view of the serious effect upon industry of local rates the costs of such work should be entirely a national charge'[79]

Times were hard right through the 1920s. In 1923 a letter came to the board from the Ministry for Health Inspector setting out the powers of the Guardians in dealing with Hunger Marches. The unemployed were expected to apply for admission and the master should be authorised to designate part of the workhouse for these casuals.

During the cold winter of 1929 when the ground was too hard for the men to be put to work digging, they chopped wood which the Master found himself unable to sell. He explained to the Guardians that it was piling up in the storerooms and they needed to put the price down. The local market was flooded with the wood from broken-up barges. George Andrews, a member of the board who owned a fleet of barges, explained that many bargemen were also out of work and that Smeed Dean had given them old barges to break up so the men were selling the firewood door to door. The company bought back the old iron recovered from the dismantling of the boats.[80]

The workhouse had one or two other sources of income. Pigs continued to be raised at the workhouse. Ten fat pigs were sold at Sittingbourne stock market in 1929.

---

[79] ibid
[80] East Kent Gazette Feb 23 1929

By this date the Guardians were showing greater flexibility in applying some of the rules, especially to facilitate employment. They allowed some illegitimate babies to remain in the workhouse without their mothers to allow the latter to gain work and make a contribution to the cost of their upkeep.

The Infirmary

It was not until 1923 that on the advice of an inspector, a fully trained head nurse was appointed. The inspector had complained that there was insufficient hot water and that modern bedsteads should be purchased for the patients. The nursery he found totally unsuitable. The Guardians could not bring themselves to spend money on the bedsteads or water, but two old cottages at the side of the workhouse were done up as the nursery and they decided to create accommodation for the extra nurses they needed by converting an unused ward and putting in windows facing the street.

The nursing staff in 1936. Sister Thorold stands third from the left in the back row. Nurse Caroline Lashbrook is at the end of the back row on right and in front of her is Nurse Poulton (Courtesy of Mr Littlewood)

The First World War

During the First World War many workhouses were commandeered by the military; this happened early at the Sheppey workhouse, so that by September 1914 the Milton clerk to the Guardians had heard from the Sheppey Union that within the month their inmates must be sent to neighbouring institutions. Milton replied that they could take 37 in the infirmary and 50 in the institution. So by November there were 268 inmates plus the 60 children in the two houses and over 30 casuals. Christmas was still celebrated well though with roast beef, plum pudding and a pint of beer for each adult and

2oz of dry tea for each female and 1 oz of tobacco for each male, with chicken for the officers.

By autumn, 1915, the Guardians were complaining that the Sheppey inmates were costing more to maintain than the actual reimbursement. As for the inmates they wanted to return to the island to be nearer home.[81]

At the outbreak of war Hulbard and Sons, the Sittingbourne High Street grocer with the contract for supplying the workhouse, had anticipated difficulties in fulfilling their contract and were warning of shortages of some items. In 1915 the Guardians decided in view of the shortages caused by the war to grow all the food they could on union land, not just the usual potatoes. They asked permission from the Kent Education Committee to send boys aged 12-14 to work on the farms.

During that same year Dr George Willan resigned as medical officer for the Milton district to serve in the forces. He was awarded a gratuity of £15 by the Guardians and Mr J. Crundwell the housemaster of Langley House asked for permission to join the army. It was decided his post was to be kept open for him and his wife was to do his job.

The war brought a strangely titled concert to the inmates. It was the Clara Butt-Kennerley Rumford Concert Party which had been organised in aid of distressed musicians who were thrown out of work because of the war. Five artistes arrived from the station at Sittingbourne in a carriage ordered by the Guardians. A piano was borrowed for the occasion and wheeled into the dining hall which was the largest room in the building. There is no record of how the concert was received by the inmates.

---

[81] East Kent Gazette August 1915

The war brought peoples' distrust of anyone who might be a foreigner to the fore, and the Master suffered because his surname was Baum. In 1915 he wrote in great distress to the Guardians as follows:-

> Gentlemen
>
> I beg to inform you that since Friday I have been subjected to great annoyance by being stigmatised as a German and have been reported to the Military and police as having signalled to the Zeppelins from the Infirmary window.
>
> I think I have found the author of these statements and have instituted legal proceedings but I respectfully ask for your sympathetic support. I need hardly say that all statements of this kind are utterly false and I would point out that in less than two minutes after the fall of the bombs I was in telephone communication with the two homes and personally visited all of them within half an hour of the raid. I have since been on duty until two or three in the morning.
>
> I am responsible as head for the Institution, Langley House and Church House and will continue to do as I have always done my duty but I should like it publicly announced that I have the full confidence of the Board. This I am sure would greatly assist me in my arduous duties.
>
> Yours obediently
> W.R.Baum

Baum was asked to make a personal statement to the Guardians in which he stated that he was the son of parents and grandparents who had always lived in

England, did not know the German language, and his sympathies were entirely anti-German. The Board recorded their entire confidence in William Baum's loyalty and he remained Master until 1925 when his wife died.

Some workhouses which had been taken over by the military never re-opened, their inmates remaining in neighbouring institutions.

When peace was celebrated nationally in 1919 the Local Government Board authorised Guardians everywhere to pay for some entertainment for workhouse inmates and for those on out-door relief, to have their money doubled for a week. The inmates enjoyed food as if it were Christmas day and the Co-op choir came to sing.

Removal Orders

It is shocking to find that well into the twentieth century, the poor could still be returned to their place of legal settlement by the magistrates if they started to claim help and became a burden on the rates. The principle of legal settlement came from the centuries old Settlement Act which had laid down that people who needed parish relief could be returned to their parish of birth. The 1834 Poor Law act had simply changed this to the union area of their birth.

The Milton Guardians rigid policy of not granting out-relief to those not resident in their area came under criticism from the more flexible Maidstone Guardians in 1915. Their criticism came out of the case of a widow with four children who was living in Maidstone but whose legal settlement was Milton. The Maidstone Guardians repeatedly asked for her to be granted out-relief by the Milton Board of Guardians. The woman was living with her elderly parents and earning eleven shillings a week and with the six shillings given her by the Maidstone Guardians had just been able to cope. As the Milton Guardians refused, the woman would have to move back to Milton losing her job and the help of her parents in looking after the children. She would then have to enter the workhouse. Milton Guardians refused to reconsider.

Other cases cropped up from time to time. In 1923 William Collins aged 57, a pauper of Southampton, was removed to the Milton workhouse because Sittingbourne was his legal settlement. In 1927 Thomas Hughes aged 11, a boy with the double misfortune of being both illegitimate and disabled, was living in the East India Dock Road, Poplar, with his grandfather Thomas Hughes when their circumstances deteriorated. They were moved to the Milton workhouse as their place of settlement was Sittingbourne where they had once lived at the White Hart Inn in Crown Quay Lane.[82]

Vagrants

At the beginning of the twentieth century the numbers of vagrants arriving at the entrance of the workhouse was increasing. In 1907 a committee of the Guardians looked into the question of how more beds could be provided for them.[83] There was a cottage in the grounds of the workhouse which was used to store the fruit and onions grown on the institution's land. The committee suggested

---

[82] CKS G / Mi AS
[83] CKS G /MiAM22

that this be adapted to take fifteen male beds, whilst an upper floor could be inserted into the barn on the workhouse field to store the onions. The existing ward could fit in more beds and a cubicle was to be provided in the vagrant's ward for inmates suffering from 'the itch'. Then the Master and Matron's sleeping quarters were to be adapted to hold twenty female casuals. This would then entail the board room becoming the new quarters for the Master. The committee completed their report by recommending that a new board room be built on the field opposite the workhouse. All was approved apart from the new building, instead the money was to be saved by the board holding their meetings in the Town Hall at Sittingbourne, and this they began to do the very next week.

Tramps continued to walk the country in large numbers during the 1920s and in 1929 between 20 and 40 a week arrived at Milton to seek a night's sleep in the workhouse. I have been told by local people, (who were children in the town), of how the tramps would hide any few possessions they had in the hedges near the workhouse before going in, for fear of them being stolen by the other vagrants. One recalled finding a pair of gloves with a sixpence in it and another a pair of slippers. They remember too how they would hear the workhouse bell ringing in the evening to give warning of locking up time. Some of the tramps were regulars well known in the town and had their nick-names such as 'Peanut Dolly' and 'Four and six'. A number of them still picked up fleas on their travels as Mr Littlewood of Sittingbourne recalls. Each time his father visited to the workhouse to service the boilers, one or two would manage to make their way home with him.

Unusual Cases

Occasionally the poor were still helped to emigrate and Patience Horton was one of these, she had five children and lived at Ship Yard, East Street in Sittingbourne. Her husband had gone on ahead to Canada to make a new life for the family and in 1906 the Guardians instigated enquiries as to what his situation there was before deciding how much help to give.[84] Eventually they got enough support to allow them to emigrate.

In 1924 Mr Charles Brunger of Oswego New York, wrote to the Guardians about his niece Rose Williams who had been in the girls home in Milton since 1914 owing to the inability of her parents to care for her. She was now 16, Mr Brunger was keen to adopt Rose and sent a ticket for her voyage. References as to the good character of Mr Brunger were applied for and sent, and Rose set sail from Southampton for her new life in 1925.[85]

The Regime is Softened

During the 1920s the yard walls were lowered (finally coming down in 1931), and the inmates were no longer segregated. This was symptomatic of a general softening of the attitude towards them. In the later years of the institution there was also far more contact with the community outside. This process had begun before the First World War and the contacts then grew. In 1905 the inmates were invited to Sittingbourne and Milton

---

[84] CKS G/MiAM22
[85] CKS G/MiAZ2

Gardeners Society and also attended the Sittingbourne Co-op sports day which became an annual outing. In January 1929 the Master reported that the boys of the Meccano club had entertained the workhouse boys, the Rev. Allen and St Michaels Sports Club had also entertained the children. Gifts of fruit had been received for the infirmary patients from the Milton Women's Conservative Association and two pictures from one of the Guardians, Mr George Andrews, for the children's homes.

A long list of contributions by local businesses to the Christmas festivities at the workhouse was printed in the local paper. It included toys given by Woolworth's, crackers, cakes, sweets and tobacco given by Sittingbourne Co-operative Society and oranges from Hulburds. The Guardians contributed individual gifts such as sweets and toys or money towards the food. Father Christmas visited the children and there were gifts on the tree for every child. Games were played into the evening.[86] What a contrast it all makes with the first Christmas in the institution.

That same year in July, over sixty of the elderly residents were taken to Margate for the day using funds raised from a sale of needlework; they were accompanied by Matron and the Rev. and Mrs Woodruff.

At the same time as contacts with the outside world had been built up the interior of the workhouse began to look a little more comfortable. One such improvement was the purchase of eight hearth rugs and an armchair for the infirmary in 1919 together with blinds for the windows.

---

[86] East Kent Gazette Jan 12 1929

By 1930 there was a wireless in the day room and infirmary.

The Workhouse Becomes the Institution

The terms workhouse and paupers had been dropped from official use after the First World War and replaced by inmate and institution. In 1929 the Local Government Act was passed, which meant the end of the existing Boards of Guardians. Unions were disbanded and their responsibilities taken over by committees of County Councils who would handle the sick, the elderly, children, the insane and the poor through a variety of special authorities.

However many workhouses continued to operate much as before. The Faversham Union for example had not even been modernised enough by 1945 to have anything other than coal fires, and the high dividing walls had not been removed.[87] All of which made Milton look quite progressive by comparison. The use of the word workhouse remained general although they had officially been named Poor Law Institutions for some years.

The Milton board of Guardians were kept pretty much in the dark by the county council as to the future of the workhouse. They did not know by January 1930 whether it was to continue to hold the same mixture of inmates or whether in the April it was to become a hospital.[88] This made them hesitate as to whether to move the pig sties as

---

[87] Memories of Lionel Lewis last master of the Faversham Union.
[88] East Kent Gazette Jan 18 1930

requested by the council who had recently erected houses close by and were worried that rats from the sties might infest them. If the institution were to become purely a hospital the Guardians felt that pigs might no longer be kept! At last at the end of January the County Council replied to a letter of enquiry form the board saying: 'I think it likely that your institution will be used for very much the same purpose after March 31st.'

The Guardians met for the last time at the end of March and the paid officers of the institution such as the Master and relieving officer were informed that they should carry on their duties as before, except that the board of Guardians would be superseded by the Public Assistance Committee acting through the Guardians Committee. Edward Handcock the chairman of the Guardians, was presented with the clock which had long stood in the board room.[89]

There was a reorganisation so that boards of guardians were grouped together and those for Milton now met as the 'Faversham and District Guardians Committee'. This covered the Sheppey, Milton and Faversham institutions and they met in rotation in Sittingbourne, Faversham and Sheerness. In fact many of the same Guardians were to serve on the committee and they carried on much the same tasks. In some counties very little work was given to the Guardians committees other than out-relief. But in Kent the detailed management of the institutions was left to the Guardians.[90] Nevertheless, the Public Assistance Committee was determined to improve and make them more comfortable and humane. Some institutions were changed to cater for one type of inmate only, and so some

---

[89] East Kent Gazette Mar 29 1930

[90] History of the Kent County Council 1889-1974, E. Melling

became hospitals or old peoples homes, but Milton remained a mixed institution. Numbers on out-relief in the county rose as a policy was followed of admitting fewer able-bodied people to the institutions.

As a first step, to see what needed doing, the public assistance officer for the county, with the county medical officer, wrote a report on all the institutions in Kent in 1930.[91] In order to do this they visited each site. Their opinion of the Milton building was damning:

> 'All the old buildings except the infirmary are dark and low-pitched. We think that ultimately they must be condemned...it would not be worth spending any money. The young women's ward for instance is dark and unsuitable. The old women's ward is long and narrow and on one side looks into the yard and on the other the windows are opaque glass. It is not cheerful.'

One of the few buildings of which they heartily approved was the infirmary where there was space for 80 patients.

After all it was not found feasible to demolish the workhouse building for it was needed too much and so the County Council took the next best option which was to spend a great deal of money to try to make the place more suitable for its use. The heating system was transformed for £5000 and toilets, baths and sinks installed to the tune of £3000. Easy chairs were purchased for the staff rooms in 1931 and bedside tables for the infirmary. The yards were gradually transformed into gardens.

---

[91] CKS CC/R28/1/1

In spite of many improvements made since it was built, the building could still appear daunting. Mr Moore of Teynham remembers that when he had just left school in the 1930s he went to the workhouse with the electrician he worked for and found the infirmary a grim, smelly place with long silent wards close-packed with beds.

An inspector in 1930 criticised the casual wards for having no bedsteads, just hammocks which were little used the men preferring to sleep on the wooden floors.[92] The Guardians' reply to this criticism was that a previous inspector had recommended hammocks to ease the overcrowding. The regulations for casuals changed in 1930 and they no longer had to break stone but could work for 8 hours on the land, chop wood or do cleaning. However, punishments for damaging the property of the institution remained severe: a vagrant was arrested for destroying a shirt belonging to the ward and sentenced to ten days hard labour. Four young men absconded from the garden in 1931. Caught just down the road they were sentenced to 14 days in prison.

New brick pig sties were erected on the union field across the road further from the building and pigs continued to be fattened on the food which the inmates left.

Children who had been many years in care in the institution and had started their first job, were allowed to come back to stay for their holidays. These were twelve and fourteen year old with nowhere else to go. This happened a number of times in the 1930s. Matron went on annual visits to the girls who had left the institution to become maids in London and reported back as to whether they had settled well, so some interest in the girls

---

[92] CKS C/PA/Fa/1/1

was maintained. Those still in Church House and Langley House began to be taken to Dymchurch holiday camp for a fortnight in the summer. As to the adult inmates those who were well enough were taken for a day out to Margate. The staff were all now entitled to regular paid holidays.

In the midst of the Great Depression in 1930 the unemployed were required to work for the public assistance money given to them. Eight hours of digging, wheeling soil or wood chopping at the discretion of the Master was prescribed. In return a married man with no children was given ten shillings and sixpence a week on a scale rising up to fifteen shillings for a man with six children.

The town of Milton was growing larger, council houses had been built close to the institution and children from these new homes, and their dogs regularly trespassed in the grounds so a six foot high fence was erected to keep them out.

The history of the Milton union workhouse mirrors that of workhouses all over England. It is a story of harsh dealings with the poor, which over the years was softened by more compassion and care, as it was realised nationally by those in authority that poverty should not be treated as a crime.

AFTER WORD 1948-1990

The Building Becomes a Hospital

In its last years the building became a geriatric hospital under the auspices of the newly created National Health Service, coming totally under health service control in 1964. A new two-storey ward building was erected by the N.H.S. During the 1950s Myra Scott of Lynsted worked as a nurse in the hospital under a very strict Matron, Mrs Pittock. Matron and her husband lived in the building, in the old quarters of the Master and Matron, and her husband undertook maintenance. The wards were still long and dark, with beds close together. There were no lifts as yet and so patients had to be carried to the upstairs wards.

By the 1970s when Myra was working as a district nurse in Milton, the townspeople still dreaded going into the building, even though it had been a long stay geriatric hospital since 1964, they still regarded it as the workhouse. As was the norm then, patients remained in the hospital until they died. This changed during the 1980s when occupational therapy and physiotherapy helped some of the patients to be able once again to carry out the tasks of daily life at home.

In its last 20 years the hospital did become much loved locally and there was surprise and protest when its closure was announced, especially as it was not long since a new chapel and canteen had been built. Much equipment had been donated to the hospital by local charities to provide better care for the patients, and in addition a League of Friends for Milton and Keycol Hospitals had been supporting the hospital for more than

20 years. Patients regularly sat out in the garden in the summer and those who were able were taken on trips in the mini-bus. The food was good and was all cooked on the premises. In its last years there were 130 on the staff and 135 beds for patients.

A happy group of patients and nurses in the garden during the 1980s (courtesy Mrs Hodges)

It was not until April 1990 that the last patients finally left the building, leaving the remaining staff to clear out all the equipment and shred files. A service of thanksgiving had been held in the chapel to mark the closure and the stained glass window and other fittings were taken to Keycol hospital to form the basis of a new chapel there. Times had changed and long term hospital care was no longer recommended for the elderly. Many of the patients returned to the care of relatives in line with the current philosophy of care in the community, others went to Sheppey Hospital or nursing homes.

Various plans for the redevelopment of the site were considered, some of which envisaged retaining part of the original building converted into housing, but in the end all was demolished and flats were built on the site.

Appendices
Appendix 1 - List of Masters

Oliver Alderton	1835-1842
William Cobbold	1842-1862
Mr Howlett	1862-1864
Edmund Weekley	1864-1870
Job Harrison	1870-1871
Mr Fallon	1871-1872
Richard Doble Kent	1872-1875
Mr Hanson	1875-1877
Herbert Black	1877-1903
Edward Croucher	1903-1912
William Baum	1912-1925
Albert Bricknell	1925 to end of institution

Several of these men were promoted to Master from other appointments at the workhouse. Edmund Weekley was the schoolmaster before becoming Master. Edward Croucher was porter then relieving officer and collector before his promotion. William Baum too began at Milton as relieving officer.

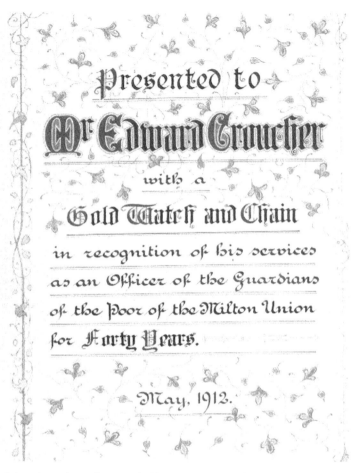

This is the beautifully written front page of a testimonial given to Edward Croucher by the Guardians on his retirement (Courtesy of V. Fox)

Appendix 2 - Some lists of Board of Guardians
The first Board of Guardians 1835

John Maxwell Tylden	chairman (Milstead)
William Bland jnr	Hartlip
George Cobb	Bredgar
William Creed Fairman	ex officio
James Fullager	Milton
William Gascoyne	Bapchild (vice chairman)
Thomas Harnett jnr	Newington
Robert Hinde	Milton
Edward Homewood	Tunstall
John Jackson	Lower Halstow
Thomas Knight	Bobbing
Charles Lake	Rodmersham
James Lake	Tong
John Marden	Iwade
George Monk Tracy (Snr.)	Murston
George Monk Tracy (Jnr.)	Sittingbourne
William Slater	Sittingbourne
Edward Strouts	Kingsdown
Thomas Wakeley	Rainham
John Walter	Borden
William Walter	Upchurch

Guardians on the board 1899-1900

Thomas Bensted	Murston
Charles Burley	Sittingbourne
Eustace Craig	Milton
William Cremer	Sittingbourne
George Dean	Sittingbourne
William Drake	Bobbing
John Epps	Sittingbourne
Alex Fairweather	Sittingbourne
George Goodhew	Bredgar
Henry Greensted	Tunstall
Alfred Harnett	Newington
William Jarrett	Kingsdown
Richard Locke	Hartlip
George Mattocks	Rainham
Sidney Ray	Milton
Frederick Seager	Upchurch
John Seager	Borden
Henry South	Halstow
James Stewart	Rainham
Albert J. Thomas	Rodmersham
Richard Tylden	Milstead

The workhouse staff then comprised:

Herbert Black	Master
Sarah Ann Black	Matron
Florence Hoadley	Industrial trainer
Henry Hayter	Boys warder
Venus Harnden	Assistant Matron

The Guardians in 1920

Esther Andrews	Sittingbourne
George Andrews	Murston
George Dean	Sittingbourne
Thomas Goodhew	Bredgar
John Filmer	Milton
Richard Hadaway	Sittingbourne
Edward Handcock	Sittingbourne
Alice Harvey	Milton
Alfred Hinge	Borden
William Hooker	Milstead
George Quinnell	Rainham
Henry South	Lower Halstow
Stanley Stevens	Newington
Harry Triplow	Iwade
Richard Wakeley	Rainham
Seymour Wakeley	Upchurch
Walter Wood	Tong

Appendix 3 - Chairmen of the Board of Guardians

<u>Sir John Maxwell TYLDEN</u> (1787-1866) In reality the first chairman of the union since the Rev. Poore resigned almost as soon as appointed, Tylden was chairman from 1835-1866. The Tylden family had been Lords of the Manor of Milstead since the seventeenth century. Sir John was the eldest son born at Milstead. His brother was William Burton Tylden. Sir John enlisted in the army in 1804 as ensign in the 43rd foot. He served in South America, India and the Peninsular War in 1813 and in America in 1814. He was knighted that year and continued in the army until his retirement in 1825 as lieutenant colonel. He was one of the leaders of the Liberal party in East Kent, and served as a Justice of the Peace. The author of the history of Milstead, Lena Jordan writes 'Sir John was perhaps the most loved Tylden and endeared himself to young and old, rich and poor. The 1835 riots show him trying to be fair and diplomatic to the upholding of the law as well as the poorer villagers'.

Sir John naturally dominated the Guardians who served with him, after all he was used to giving orders and was socially far their superior since most of them were farmers or business men.

He died at Milstead in 1866.

<u>Major Richard KNIGHT</u> When Knight died in 1891 the board sent condolences to his family 'who for 43 years wisely and faithfully was a Guardian. He was honest and energetic in the performance of his duties.

Richard TYLDEN ex-officio Guardian. In 1891 he was elected chairman which he remained until his death in 1909. He was Sir John's nephew and the inheritor of his estates. A classical scholar and a musical man, he was popular in Milstead.

Appendix 4 - The inmates in 1861 on census night

As listed in the 1861 census (RG9 528 ,133-135) The only other detail given in the census is whether the inmates are married, widowed or single.

Name	age	where born
Rebecca Fentril	67	Milton
Amelia Wickens	34	"
Charles "	6	"
Elizabeth Marden	33	Lower Halstow
Mary A. Vant	8	"
Sarah A. Marden	6	Milton
James Grigsby	81	Bredgar
William Baker	71	Kingsdown
Frances "	91	Lower Halstow
George H. Whitnall	11	Borden
Henry H. "	19	"
Ann Sellen	33	Brompton
Mary A. "	4	Middlesex St Georges
William Bryant	49	Borden
Sarah Wildish	50	Upchurch
Matilda Cork	41	Greenwich
Eliza "	18	"
Emma "	9	"

Georgiana Cork	4	Greenwich
Ellen Earl	17	Bredgar
Thomas Taylor	67	Milton
Henry Clarke	14	Hartlip
Ann "	17	"
Henry Whitehead	80	Eynsford
Charles Lockyer	6	Iwade
Phoebe "	3	Milton
Margaret Jenner	72	Ramsgate
Thomas Sutton	72	Canterbury
Elizabeth Chrisfield	34	Milton
William Horton	12	Sittingbourne
Jane Sage	12	Milton
Sarah Capleden	24	"
George Milloway	76	"
Jane Eagle	9	Canterbury
Sarah Aldridge	46	Chatham
Isaac "	9	Old Brompton
Ester "	6	"
Henry Heyton	21	Milton
RichardFisher	74	Murston
John Tassel	83	Newington
James Anderson	11	"

John Anderson	10	Newington
Mary Taylor	83	Gillingham
Charles Trice	12	Rainham
William Mole	10	"
Frederick "	7	"
Stephen Nichols	41	"
Jane Miles	21	"
Robert Featherstone	20	Hollingbourne
William Thomas	21	Rodmersham
John Horton	64	"
William Baker	69	Adisham
Francis A. Annings	68	Sittingbourne
William Rose	10	"
Emily Ruck	25	"
Eliza Welby	46	"
Maria Pound	49	"
William Higgins	83	Kingsdown
John Wood	27	Sittingbourne
Robert "	33	"
Elizabeth Hall	43	Sheerness
Richard "	11	Milton
George Phipps	87	"
Maria Ambrose	45	Boxley

Sampson Scamp	87	Loose
Hannah Hubbard	15	Upchurch
Thomas "	12	Surrey Camberwell
Amelia "	10	"
Caroline "	8	"
Susan "	7	"
James White	71	Stone
Henrietta Scamp	87	Dartford
Emma Baker	21	Milton
Charlotte Benshaw	15	Upchurch
John "	11	Milton
Elizabeth "	8	"
Mary Ann Horton	69	Sittingbourne
Catherine Milliner	90	Milton
Edwin Saxby	72	"
Hannah Cheel	50	Baddlesmere
Mary Ann "	11	Bredgar
Henry Rickwood	61	Dartford
Esther Browning	19	Broad Oak
George W "	3wk	Milton
John Pelehurst	60	France British subject
William Box	64	Milton
Thomas Reeves	64	Nottingham Castle Gate

Appendix 5 - The records of the Milton Union Workhouse

A substantial number of records survive in the care of the Centre for Kentish Studies at Maidstone and many of these are on microfilm. The series catalogue number is G/Mi.

The documents include the Minute books of the Guardians' meetings, the records of vaccination and financial records. There are registers of births which took place inside the institution from 1866 and deaths from 1893. Then there are the admission and discharge books. These records mostly continue until 1930.

After 1930 there are County Council public assistance records C/Pa which continue until the National Health service began in 1948.

At the National Archives at Kew there is the correspondence of the Poor Law Commissioners with the Guardians. This is the MH12 series.

Bibliography

Sittingbourne & Milton	P.Bellingham (1996)
The new poor law in the nineteenth century	D.Fraser (1976)
The early Victorians 1832-51	J.Harrison (1971)
Money or Blood	D.Hopker (1988)
Labouring life in the Victorian countryside	P.Horn (1987)
Strolling through Milstead	L. Jordan (2001)
Association of health & residential care officers, a short history	L.Lewis
The Workhouse	N. Longmate (1974)
Milton Regis Remembered	Members of the Freedom Centre (1999)
History of the Kent County Council	E.Melling (1975)
Rural life in Victorian England	G.Mingay (1976)
The workhouse: A study of poor-law buildings in England	K.Morrison (1999)
The union workhouse. A study guide for teachers and local historians	A. Reid (1994)
The relief of poverty 1834-1914	M.Rose (1986)
Faversham union workhouse: the early years	J.Stevens (2002)

Poverty and the workhouse in Victorian Britain	P.Wood (1991)
Religion and society in Kent, 1640-1914	Yates, Hume & Hastings (1994)

Index

Acremans Field, 35
Alderton
  Elizabeth, 57
  Oliver, 20, 57
Anderson, Edith, 97
Andrews, George, 101, 110
apprenticeships, 49, 97
Baker
  George, 59
  Stephen, 59
Bapchild, 14
Barnard, Richard, 42
Baum, William, 106
Bean, Elizabeth, 72
Black
  George, 28
  Herbert, 82
  John, 28
  Sarah, 82
Bland, William, 21
Bond, Rev. William, 79
Borden, 70, 84
Bowes, George, 97
Bredgar, 13, 29, 37, 58
Brewer, Rev. William, 63
brick making, 7, 35
Burley, Charles, 50, 68
Burnett, Sarah Ann, 84
Canada, 84
Carter, Charlotte, 52

Chambers, Sir Samuel, 13
cholera, 60
Chrisfield, Stephen, 49, 71
Christmas, 54, 110
Church House, 94
Cobbold
  Lucy, 32, 48
  William, 48, 55
Collins, William, 107
Cook, John, 33, 55
Cooper, John, 79
Court, Henry, 30
Crayden
  Thomas, 98
  William, 98
Croucher family, 83
Croucher, Edward, 50
Curtis
  Ann, 62
  James, 50
Dean, Susan, 28
Derbyshire, 40
Doddington, 14, 17
Durant, Edward, 79
Eason
  Hannah, 28
  John, 62
Eley, George, 65
Elliott, William, 41
Ellis, Francis, 62
emigrants, 109

English, Rev., 72
Fairman, William, 21
Fawkener, James, 62
Featherstone, James, 29
fetes, 82
Fisher, Dr, 93
Friday, Israel, 79
Fullager, William, 71
Gascoyne, William, 18
Golding, George, 38
Grayling, Mr, 58
Greaves, Rev. George, 43
Greenstreet, William, 62
Handcock, Edward, 112
Hanham, Rev. Abdiel, 78
Harker, Rev. William, 84
Harvey, Mrs Alice, 93
Head
   Sir Francis, 11, 14, 15, 21, 22, 37, 96
   Susan, 37
Heathfield, Stephen, 94
Highsted, 99
Hobbs, Jane, 42
Hoby, William, 80
Hollingbourne Union, 39, 52
Holmes, Thomas, 51
Homewood, Edward, 18
Honey, Eliza, 55
Hope, Joseph, 84
Horton, Patience, 109
Hughes, Thomas, 107

illegitimacy, 29
Imlach, Dr, 58
infectious hospital, 67
Ingram family, 84
Irons, John, 79
Johnson, Fanny, 62
Kent, Richard, 84
King, George, 77
Lambkin, Mary, 77
Langley House, 96
Lavender, John, 50
Lippingwell, James, 37
Long, Albert, 97
Maidstone, 106
Marmion, Dr Edward, 93
medical officers, 57
mentally ill, 58
Mills, Stephen, 62
Milton, 10, 20, 72, 98
Milton parish
   workhouse, 60
Milway
   George, 62
   Henry, 77
Mitchell
   Thomas, 38
   William, 80
Moon, James, 31
Moore, James, 84
Nelson, Thomas, 94
New Zealand, 84
Newman Constable, Golding, 49
oakum picking, 32

Penfold, Dr, 64, 85, 93
Peters, John, 49
Poore, Rev., 13, 18, 44
Price, John, 38
Public Assistance
   Committee, 112
Ramsgate, 50, 97
Randall, Edmund, 77
Ray, George, 57, 60, 63
Reynolds
   Charlotte, 48
   John, 48
Roberts, John, 62
Rodmersham, 17
Rossiter, Richard, 28
sanitation, 23, 67
Satteen
   George, 77
   James, 38
   John, 38
Saywell, Richard, 71
Seager
   John, 94
   Lawrence, 68
   Mary, 33
settlement, 71
Sittingbourne Co-
   operative Society, 110
Skilder, Isaac, 58
Smeed, George, 41, 50, 82
Stiles, George, 57
stone breaking, 34, 73, 98

Strouts, Walter, 72
Syfleet, Anglina, 72
Tarpe, Thomas, 70
Thomas, James, 36
Tunstall, 72, 99
Twirl, Mary, 28
Tylden
   Richard, 68
   Sir John, 16, 18, 24, 65, 68, 124
typhoid, 66
uniform, 36, 94
vaccination, 57
Vant, Elizabeth, 37, 44
Vinton, John, 16, 70
Wakelin
   James, 83
   Stephen, 83
Weatherhead, William, 43
Webb, William, 28
Welby, Daniel, 38
Weller, William, 38
Wheeler, Mary Ann, 58
White
   Elizabeth, 65
   James, 38
Willan, Dr George, 104
Williams, Rose, 109
Wills, Tom, 62
Wilson, Arthur, 94
Wood, Robert, 39
Woodruff, Rev., 110